PENNSYLVANIA

MARYLAND

DEL

Mason Neck

Cross Mountain

Shenandoah
National Park

North River
Gorge

Rappahannock
River

River

Moormans
River

Fan Mountain

James River

Richmond

Barrier
Islands

VIRGINIA

Blackwater River

North Landing River

Great Dismal Swamp

False Cape/
Back Bay

TH CAROLINA

uncommon
wealth

uncommon
wealth

essays

on Virginia's

wild places

Edited by Robert M. Riordan
Introduction by Jennifer Ackerman

Falcon® Publishing, Inc., Helena, Montana
Printed in the United States of America

2 3 4 5 6 7 8 9 0 TS 04 03 02 01 00

"And This Way the Water Comes Down at the Gorge" ©1994 by Janet Lembke. Reprinted from *Skinny Dipping* by permission of The Lyons Press, New York City.

Library of Congress Cataloging-in-Publication Data
Uncommon Wealth : essays on Virginia's wild places / edited by Robert M.
    Riordan ; introduction by Jennifer Ackerman ; illustrations by Megan Grey Rollins.
        p.   cm.
    ISBN 1-56044-915-2 (hardcover)
    1. Natural history--Virginia. I. Riordan, Robert M.
    QH105.V8U53   1999
    508.755--dc21   99-30128
                                                                                    CIP

In-house Editor: Megan Hiller
Production Editor: Larissa Berry
Copyeditor: Polly Carter-Maynard
Page Compositor: Joe Menden

Book and cover design by Michael Cutter
Jacket illustration by Peter Ring

The Nature Conservancy's share of the proceeds from this book will be used to further the Conservancy's work in Virginia.

    The Nature Conservancy is grateful to the authors for their generous donation of original work. The views expressed in these essays are the authors' own and do not necessarily represent the opinions or policies of the organization.

CONTENTS

Acknowledgments vii

About The Nature Conservancy viii

Foreword ix

Introduction xi
   by Jennifer Ackerman

New Ground

Barriers 3
   Christopher Camuto on the Barrier Islands

A Bright and Shining Swamp 11
   Ellen Dudley on the Blackwater River

Fist-Cloud at Laurel Fork 25
   Jack Wennerstrom on Laurel Fork

Christmas with Eagles: A Holi-day in Four Parts 36
   Judith Kahn on Mason Neck

Into the Great Dismal 53
   Stefan Bechtel on Great Dismal Swamp

Loss and Recompense at the Pinnacle 66
   Garvey Winegar on the Pinnacle, Clinch River

Home Ground

Forest Children 75
   Susan Tyler Hitchcock on Fan Mountain

Escape to North River Gorge 83
   Deane Winegar on North River Gorge

Seasons of Life 91
    Paul Clancy on False Cape and Back Bay

The Forest Returns 98
    Jim Crawford on Bottom Creek Gorge

A River Good Enough: On the Merits of Modest Water 109
    Donovan Webster on the Moormans River

I Write from a Mountain Farm 124
    Richard Cartwright Austin on the Clinch River

To Love a Place 130
    Chris Bolgiano on Cross Mountain

Prime Mountain Real Estate: "Best Views in the World" 138
    Eric Seaborg on Shenandoah National Park

Roots

A Mountain Retrospective: Revisiting Southwest Virginia 155
    Curtis J. Badger on Southwest Virginia

Only in the Land of Goshen 166
    Katie Letcher Lyle on Goshen Pass

Wild in the City: The Urban James River 177
    Elizabeth Seydel Morgan on the James River

Where Rare Plants Dwell 187
    Mary Reid Barrow on the North Landing River

In the Blood 195
    Walter Nicklin on the Rappahannock River

And This Way the Water Comes Down at the Gorge 205
    Janet Lembke on the Bullpasture River

About the Editor 217

ACKNOWLEDGMENTS

I am deeply grateful to the authors, each of whom donated his or her time, words, and love of nature to The Nature Conservancy for this anthology. I am equally indebted to Megan Grey Rollins for contributing her illustrations and to Peter Ring for contributing the cover art. Special thanks go to Jennifer Ackerman, Joe Barbato, Patty Housman, and Anna Lawson for their guidance in developing this project. The contributors were helped by many naturalists, conservationists, and friends, including Chuck Conley, Ches Goodall, Don Gowan, Stan Gray, Susan Lilly, M. W. Paxton, Jr., Johnny Pilcicki, Mary Jane Reyes, Diana Rock, Walt Rock, Barry Truitt, Gary Williamson, and Ralph White.

Robert M. Riordan
Director of Communications
The Nature Conservancy, Virginia Chapter

About The Nature Conservancy

The Nature Conservancy is an international, nonprofit organization dedicated to preserving the plants, animals, and natural communities that represent the diversity of life on Earth by protecting the lands and waters they need to survive. Founded in 1951, the Conservancy has protected more than 11 million acres in all 50 states and also works with partner organizations in Latin America, the Caribbean, and the Pacific to help protect more than 55 million acres outside the United States. The Conservancy owns and manages more than 1500 hundred nature preserves across America, the largest nongovernmental system of refuges in the world, and is supported by more than one million members.

In Virginia, The Nature Conservancy has protected more than 220,000 acres of wildlife habitat through more than 500 land projects, many of which are highlighted in this book. With the support of 35,000 Virginia Chapter members, the Conservancy owns and manages 31 nature preserves across the Commonwealth.

For more information, or to join The Nature Conservancy, please contact us at:

The Nature Conservancy
Virginia Chapter   Telephone: 804-295-6106
490 Westfield Road   E-mail: rriordan@tnc.org
Charlottesville, VA 22901   Website: www.tnc.org/virginia

Foreword

As a boy growing up in southeastern Virginia, many of my most important life lessons came from observing wildlife and wild places, which seemed to have the ability to speak important truths in their own way. Later, I got "educated," and realized that just as nature could speak to people, so people had important things to say about nature. I still refer to the writings of such famed eighteenth-century naturalists as John Bartram, Mark Catesby, William Byrd, and Thomas Jefferson, each of whom teaches us volumes about what wild Virginia was like centuries ago.

Much has been lost since their time, but many wild places still remain. In this anthology, twenty of Virginia's gifted writers—heirs to those early naturalists—explore some of Virginia's finest remaining natural areas. Drawing on natural history and personal experience, using humor and hope, their words help us to make sense of what we find and what we feel when we venture into the wilds.

Virginia is fortunate to have such an exceptional group of writers who call the Commonwealth home, and The Nature Conservancy is very fortunate and grateful to have received the gift of their words. Each of these essays is an original piece written for this anthology, with the authors and illustrators generously donating their work. In asking these authors to write about their favorite places, we left each one free to write whatever he or she wanted about that particular special place. Together, their diverse impressions of Virginia's wild places create a book that exceeds the sum of its parts.

Through their words, the authors have underscored the impor-
tance of the work that The Nature Conservancy does. Many of the
places you will read about in this book have been protected by The
Nature Conservancy; some are among our public lands, while others
are in private ownership. Whether in public or private hands, protecting these wild places—Virginia's greatest natural areas—matters. As
these essays reveal, it matters to our hearts, our souls, and our physical well-being. Perhaps more importantly, our will to preserve these
places says something about our relationship to the future.

It's been said that hope is, fundamentally, an orientation toward
the future. If we do not bother to save the best of what has been
passed down to us so that our children and grandchildren can also see
and experience these places, then we are giving up on the future. That
would be a denial of hope, and a denial of something very funda-
mental to our souls and our communities.

Michael Lipford
Vice President and Virginia Director
The Nature Conservancy

INTRODUCTION

Jennifer Ackerman

There was a time when a book like this one, designed to celebrate wild nature, would have been inconceivable. Settlers drifting inland from toeholds on the shores of colonial Virginia saw the wilderness as vast, desolate, intimidating. The dark mountains, deep gorges and wide rivers were obstacles to cross, full of perils, malign spirits, ruthless animals. The swamps were beds of fever, releasing noxious odors from the bowels of the earth, capable of making mankind sick. Hope, safety, progress resided in carving from fathomless nature small outposts of civilization.

But in the last two hundred years, the geometry of nature and culture has changed. Now it is the wild places that stand as outposts, pockets in a matrix of human habitation. The essays in this book plumb twenty such shards of forest, swamp, barrier island, where one can still catch a sense of wildness. Some of these landscapes are large, some small; many owe their existence to The Nature Conservancy. They are breathtaking in range, from the barrier islands in the east— young, thin, wispy strands of sand, whose energetic forms are constantly wavering, dying and being reborn like the shifting flames of a fire—to the ancient Appalachians in the west, no upstart peaks of glacial white but sweet old tree-green heights, soft folded mountains that turn you to their silence.

The essays in this book make one see and live these wild remnants.

The voices vary almost as much as the landscapes they describe. Some writers immerse themselves in country they've never seen before, visitors to strange places. Others express a love of land they've known all their lives, a homely, intimate acquaintance with places they've come to lately or with native ground imprinted from an early age. Christopher Camuto emerges from his familiar dark old woods of Appalachia to take in the wide bright horizons and raw energy of Smith Island, the "protean edge of a perpetually new world." Walter Nicklin comes home to the Rappahannock again and again, his roots affirmed by the river's meandering waters. In all kinds of encounters, nature turns up surprises that shatter preconceptions: here a Canada mayflower blooming in southern woods; there a pygmy salamander not much bigger than a baby's finger, or a blind fish, or a swamp that's no hole but a hill.

If these essays share a common thread, it is the expression of desire to take in the spirit of a wild place, to attend closely to the revelations of nature, as contributor Chris Bolgiano says, to "mind the mountain."

There may be a deep hunch here. In the last couple of decades scientists have learned of the existence of "place cells" in the human brain. These are neurons in the hippocampus, an area deep within the temporal lobes of the brain that is active not only in memory but in creating and storing maps of place, locations of food, water, nest. When an animal is in a particular place, these neurons fire in a special pattern, probably stimulated by a set of environmental cues, a rich mix of sounds, smells, sights.

I like this idea of specialized cells buried deep in our reptilian brains, cued to the traits of place, the tangy scent of saltwater, the riffle of wind in maple leaves, an eagle's flight shadowing a streak of river.

* * *

Not long ago, on a muggy sunny morning in August, I paddled the waters of Virginia's Cumberland Marsh, a small tidal marsh at a bend in the Pamunkey River, owned by The Nature Conservancy. I was looking for a plant of low profile with a bright yellow bloom, a rare member of the pea family known as sensitive joint-vetch. The plant thrives on freshwater dosed with a little salt. The brackish Cumberland, which stirs the waters of the Pamunkey and the Chesapeake Bay, offers the perfect mix. Here, about two thousand stems of sensitive joint-vetch live among the stalks of arrowhead and wild rice. To paddle about the pewtery waters searching for small blooms hidden in the marsh grass made for a lovely morning and took me out of myself, focused my eye on obscure little creatures, bright red dragonflies perched in stillness on purple arrowhead, frogs and spiders engaged in beguiling tasks—all things that firm the grasp of place on self.

A dark mood would be required to imagine threats here; and yet a developer could quickly drain, fill, bulldoze this place into oblivion. In her essay on Cross Mountain, Bolgiano tries to visualize a long-gone forest of giant chestnut oak trees from the slight specimens that her woods comprise nowadays. Damage has found the spots of wildness probed in this book; all of the writers, walking the mountain paths, rowing the rivers, reflect on injured nature, the dying hemlocks, the disappearing mussels and the strewn refuse, the river sediments laced with copper leached from factory farms, the lost native trout, as Garvey Winegar says, "too fragile for man's heavy acquaintance." What are we to make of fish kills, snail kills, lifeless bays? We are not separate from what we are destroying; we are of nature, swim like fish in it, and will die if it goes dry.

Dire warnings of impending loss can numb the mind like big numbers. But one promising thing about our species is that we make language and use it to keep the mind from going slack. The essays here are efforts to make sense of place, to pass on what is learned—as Susan Tyler Hitchcock conveys to her children the secret spots of blooming bloodroot and black cohosh—and finally to give hope. The resilience and persistence of nature uncovered in these wild places, the North River still flowing in the midst of stubborn summer drought, the return of life in Back Bay, counter the numbing arithmetic of loss.

Many of these writers find rest and restoration in these places. They speak of soaking in the tonic of air and light, of invigorating nature, soothing, refreshing, healing nature. This reliance on wild land for balm and consolation is revealed in Winegar's seeking comfort for the loss of a friend in the Pinnacle's trees and cliffs, and in Janet Lembke's giving over the ashes of her uncle to the ice-cold waters of the Bullpasture River.

There's some solid scientific evidence that nature buoys our spirits, enhances well-being, helps us recoup our physical strength, even hastens recovery from illness. Views of nature make hospitalized patients feel better. I know that looking down from a rim-ledge in the Appalachians onto the slow blue ocean of lesser summits slows my heart rate, loosens my shoulders, soothes my senses. We don't have a ghost of an idea how nature works this alchemy. But the effects of natural setting are undeniable. In her book, *The Experience of Nature*, Rachel Kaplan says that even the mere knowledge that green nature is there seems to have restorative effects, whether or not we actually dive into it.

The title of this book, *Uncommon Wealth*, is a play on Virginia's status as a body politic united for the common good. Consider that the word "wealth," which seems to put the mind off at first thought, comes down to us from the Old English word *wela*, or well-being. That's what we have here, rare natural beauty belonging to all, which gives rest and pleasure, invites outward concentration, promotes our well-being.

I don't say that if we save the birdwing pearlymussel and the lily-leaved twayblade we will remain healthy and restore our sense of linkage to the rest of creation, our humility, reverence, respect. But with these small riches out there, protected, minded, it seems to me there's hope.

Jennifer Ackerman

Jennifer Ackerman's book *Notes from the Shore* explores the natural life of the mid-Atlantic coast. Her essays and articles have appeared in *National Geographic*, the *New York Times Magazine*, and other publications.

NEW GROUND

BARRIERS
The Barrier Islands

Christopher Camuto

The typical development along the Atlantic coast . . . has been the establishment of barriers.

Bill Perry, *The Middle Atlantic Coast*

The bolt of lightning that knocked Barry Truitt back from the helm—blue sparks playing between the captain's fingertips and the aluminum wheel—was not exactly what William Wordsworth had in mind when placidly contemplating the relation of a landscape to "the quiet of the sky" in "Tintern Abbey." But if our jarring morning run through rain and heaving swells offshore of the Virginia Coast Reserve islands had not already done so, that jolt served to remind those of us on board that the world of these barrier islands was still wild with primal energy. In fact, the slender, graceful curves of beach and dune that punctuate the coast of Virginia from the southern hook of Assateague Island to Cape Charles are an expression of three forms of energy—lunar, oceanic and terrestrial forces come together to have their say as shifting landforms, the protean edge of a perpetually new world.

The names of these beautiful islands connect them with their most recent history, their history as *property*—Assawoman, Metompkin, Cedar, Parramore, Revel's, Hog, Cobb's, Little Cobb's, Wreck,

Mockhorn, Ship Shoal, Myrtle and Smith's. Smith's Island, the south-ernmost, takes us back to Captain John Smith and the Jamestown settlement, to a time when that venture was an uncertain toehold, the very beginning of the English occupation of North America. In that tantalizing book, *The Generall Historie of Virginia . . .*, Smith gives us our first glimpse of "the Easterne shore" and the southernmost of Virginia's barrier islands: "There is but one entrance by Sea into this Country, and that is at the mouth of a very goodly Bay, 18. or 20. myles broad . . . . The north Cape is called Cape Charles, in honour of the worthy Duke of Yorke. The Isles before it, Smith's Isles, by the name of the discoverer."

piping plover

Smith was apparently referring to what are now known as Fisherman's and Smith's Islands, both of which are drawn with care on the map that William Hole produced for Smith back in London. The well-known Smith map of 1612 also charts, with less topographic clarity, what may be Myrtle and Ship Shoal and other fragments of salt marsh. Smith's Isles are thus among the first-named landforms of the English settle-ment of America. It took more than a century before the other barrier islands appeared on maps, sporting a wild variety of names, but it is difficult to find a colonial map—English, French, Spanish or Dutch—that does not show "Smith's Isles."

When Smith took seven gentlemen and seven soldiers on "the discovery of the Bay of Chesapeake" in the summer of 1608, he touched again on the islands he named for himself, but does not describe them; bent on exploring the bay, he apparently went no further up the coast on the ocean side. Elsewhere in *The Generall Historie* there are references to the abundance of fish in and around the islands, to the temporary location of a salt house on Smith's Island in 1621, to the presence of deer on the island and to the grazing of "Hogges." Smith's Island becomes more prominent two centuries later, when George Washington Parke Custis, step-grandson of the first president, used it for grazing sheep. It emerges quite clearly when Custis's son-in-law, Robert E. Lee, ventures to Smith's Island in the spring of 1832 and drafts a detailed letter to his father-in-law about the island's natural resources and economic prospects.

Except for the current version of the Smith's Island lighthouse, the weight of all that history wasn't visible when I waded ashore on the southwest tip of the island to begin a three-day walking tour of the islands in June of 1998. Neither was the storm front that had hammered us on the boat ride from Hog Island. The trailing edge of dark clouds was moving briskly to the north, leaving a fair day in its wake. My companions' task that week was to gather data on colonial nesting shorebirds, the twenty-fifth year of that important annual survey of island bird life. I was set ashore to take in the spirit of the place, not a simple task, especially for a writer who has been preoccupied with the dark cove forests of the southern Appalachians for the better part of the last decade. Although I had lived for two years on the Eastern Shore in the late 1970s, and loved salt marshes as much as I loved mountain balds, the subtle landscape of the barrier islands was as difficult to get a purchase on as a desert would have been. A forest is all foreground. The world of the barrier islands is, at first glance, all horizon.

But I knew that landscapes come into focus through the forms of life they encourage—a bear in a forest, a deer in a woodlot, a fox at the pasture's edge. I walked the beach and while sun, wind and salt air weathered me back into the grain of a once-familiar landscape, I felt the ratio of my forested expectations shift. A living ocean chanted restlessly on the wet sands, a sea breeze rattled the bayberry and wax-myrtle thickets that constitute a climax forest on Smith's Island, a gull-billed tern hawked the marsh for insects, oystercatchers and royal terns hung in the air while laughing gulls mocked overhead like crows. And though there was nothing so dense as the tangled understory of an old-growth forest at my feet, there was, it turned out, a world to see in the dunes of each barrier island that I had the opportunity to visit.

To the piping plover, Smith's Island is a welcome refuge for nest-ing, not a barrier. Here and there among midbeach sands stabilized by the roots of sea rocket were the small nests of this diminutive, nearly invisible bird. Birders are almost always excellent teachers, and with the help of my companions, I learned to see a piping plover by ear, listening for the thin reed of its voice in order to locate a wind-blown dusting of sand and seashell that turned out to be a running bird. I rather enjoyed the metamorphosis, although not every wind-blown tumult turned into a bird. I learned the discipline of walking with utmost care, not to avoid a sluggish timber rattler, but to keep from destroying nests of eggs no more visible than the birds that laid them. Once I learned how to see piping plovers and their nests, I had one way of looking at this gentle barrier of sand, one way of looking *into* it so that I could wrap its wide, mind-numbing horizon of sky and ocean around specific images.

On Ship Shoal, I looked beyond the rusted fragments of exploded shells left from target practice during World War II to see the nests of least terns. Unlike the piping plover, which relies on its protective coloration and barely audible call, least terns gather and declare them-selves aggressively, as the whole clan of terns tends to do. The least tern is the most beautiful of its kind—a graceful sliver of the idea of the species—and the art of its nest is a degree finer than that of the piping plover, if such a difference can be measured: two sand-colored, inch-long eggs in a circular depression perhaps three inches in diameter. The depression, fainter than the redd of a brook trout in the gravel of a mountain stream, was lined with bits of shell, ghost-crab claws and tiny oyster drills—the merest gesture toward creating a place in the world for new life. Anything more elaborate would attract attention. Everything on these islands must lie low.

The discreet use of beach habitat by plovers and terns contrasted sharply with the showy concert of bird life attracted to the groundsel trees and marsh elders at Clubhouse Point. A heronry is as cosmopolitan as a city, a cultured place that gathers a great diversity of life, variations on the theme of stilt-legged shorebirds. Cattle egrets and glossy ibis, migrants from Africa by way of South America, rubbed elbows with great egrets, snowy egrets and white ibis. The familiar great blue, little blue and green herons mingled with tricoloreds as well as yellow-crowned and black-crowned night herons. Nearly every hummock of vegetation hid a nest of gleaming white eggs or a pile of fuzzy, limp young barely conscious of the enormous world into which they had just been hatched.

And finally, I walked Metompkin Island, a pristine skein of land held together on the sea-side by beach grass, mustard and goldenrod and on the bay-side by emerald fields of *Spartina patens,* that low marsh grass so essential to the ecology of the Coast Reserve. I listened again for piping plovers between the thrum of the surf in one ear and the buffeting of wind in the other. I strained to see what has evolved to be invisible and learned to distinguish males from females by way of their pronounced neckband. Metompkin, more than any of the other islands I visited, was full of the poetics of nesting bird life. Piping-plover nests lay here and there on the sand, bare to the universe, so vulnerable that I wondered how this species keeps itself in being. There were gull nests made of dried vegetation, mostly straws of dried-out *patens* stems casually arranged to hold two or three hefty, mottled eggs. And a colony of black skimmers, sleeker and more dignified than the gulls, had carved out a nesting territory of its own on the inner edge of a foredune. Finally, near the northern end of Metompkin, a female Wilson's plover revealed itself in the act of stashing her young in marsh grass.

A great many creatures depend on the subtle landscape of the barrier islands, and nearly all of them are in motion—only momentarily where you last saw them. A good deal of life overlaps there: piping plovers at the southernmost extreme of their range share beach with Wilson's plovers nesting as far north as they venture. The domestic barn owls and purple martins that have taken up residence at the Hog Island Coast Guard Station might cross paths on occasion with wild pelagic travelers—gannets, shearwaters or petrels. Diamondback terrapins come ashore to lay eggs in the same sand where gulls and skimmers nest. These barriers are patient collectors of life from distant epochs. A mastodon skull and a walrus tusk have been unearthed from them, and on this excursion, two fossilized whale vertebrae lodged in the sands of Assawoman Island came to hand. Storms also toss up archaeological treasures from the continental shelf—hammer stones, celts, points and knives from villages inundated long ago by the rising ocean. And the barrier islands themselves move. In fact, they are among the most mobile landforms on earth. They migrate as surely, if more slowly, than the birds that nest on their backs. And beyond that foreground I learned to watch with care, all that windblown, primordial space remained to be pondered—the competing horizons of ocean and sky linked by the moon's dictation of tides that rise and fall silently in the marshes and mumble distinctly on the shore. Slender as the barrier islands are, in the end they seemed to me more the center of something than an edge.

"We must look a long time before we can see," Henry David Thoreau reminds us in his essay "Natural History of Massachusetts," and the shorebird survey is a good example of the kind of discovery that still awaits the visitor to these islands four centuries after their appearance on European maps. If the first explorers left us less detail about the wildlife of the islands than we might now want, my dedicated companions—Barry Truitt, Bill Williams, Ruth Beck, Michael Beck, Bill Akers and Jerry Via—missed nothing. The diversity of life they recorded makes for a heartening litany—brown pelicans, great herons, little blue herons, green herons, tricolored herons, great egrets, snowy egrets, cattle egrets, yellow-crowned night herons, black-crowned night herons, glossy ibis, white ibis, royal terns, sandwich terns, Caspian terns, common terns, gull-billed terns, least terns, Forster's terns, black skimmers, laughing gulls, herring gulls, great black-backed gulls—all distributed among a wide expanse of sea, sand and sky. In addition to these colonial species were the beach-nesting piping plovers, Wilson's plovers and oystercatchers. And, in passing, we noted willets, horned larks, common nighthawks, northern harriers, gannets far south of where they should be, two peregrine falcons keeping watch from an old Coast Guard tower on the south end of Cobb Island and a barn owl that was raising seven hissing young in an oil drum on Hog Island.

Bring any group of specialists to the barrier islands—experts in marine life, intertidal-zone species, crustaceans, grasses, wildflowers, plants, trees, insects—and each would build an equally impressive list of the life of this complex, subtle world. Now that the islands are protected from development by the stewardship of the Virginia Coast Reserve, and preserved as much as anything on this abused planet can be, we can look at them, study them, contemplate them. We can, as Thoreau suggested a century and a half ago, go about the challenging business of discovering "the discovery."

The commitment to preserve these islands recognizes the opportunity these so-called barriers represent—the rare opportunity to make contact with a wild coastal landscape free of the soul-destroying clutter of "development" that always leaves this over-crowded world a smaller place. Some of us need these barriers as much as do plovers and terns, egrets and ibis, diamondbacks and loggerheads. And there is much to be learned from re-establishing a psychological attachment to the world of wrackline, beach and dune and from experiencing the primordial relationship to sky and ocean that only this extraordinary landscape affords. The preservation of this edge of North America provides an extraordinary opportunity for human beings and wildlife alike and leaves intact a place where wind and weather may have their say and where the moon decides, at any moment, where an ocean ends and a continent begins.

Christopher Camuto is the author of *A Fly Fisherman's Blue Ridge* (Henry Holt, 1990), *Another Country: Journeying Toward the Cherokee Mountains* (Henry Holt, 1997), and *Hunting from Home*, forthcoming from W. W. Norton. He is the book review columnist for *Audubon* and *Gray's Sporting Journal* and writes the "Watersheds" column for *Trout*. He has taught writing, American literature, and Native American literature at the University of Virginia and at Washington and Lee University. He makes his home in Rockbridge County, Virginia.

The Nature Conservancy began protecting land on the Eastern Shore barrier islands in 1969. Today the Virginia Coast Reserve encompasses forty-five thousand acres on fourteen barrier islands.

A Bright and Shining Swamp
Blackwater River

Ellen Dudley

The coastal plain baked in a stifling July-in-April estival somno-lence—plowed fields dried to a pale dun, bold creeks parched to a slow flow, trees clothed in summer's matronly greens. This was the Tidewater flatland—predictable and tame, sedated by sun and heat, not the sort of country that might produce a surprise, no hint of the startling contrast just beyond the riparian tree line. Yet behind that leafy curtain was another world, and soon we, like Alice through the looking glass, would pass from the ordinary into the extraordinary.

Nature's landscape transitions are usually gentle, a slow and subtle blending of features that ushers in a new topography. But occasion-ally there's an anomaly, a dramatic juxtaposition, a change so abrupt that you blink at the wondrous contrast so concealed within familiar contours. I encountered just such a metamorphosis before, hiking across Utah's high desert country where the flat sage-and-sand plain seemed to stretch endlessly to the far horizon. Suddenly that hori-zontal, monochromatic world ended at the edge of a precipice, and a new vertical and polychromatic world opened up below, a vast canyon filled with red rocks, pink sands, purple primroses, and green cotton-woods.

But that was the larger-than-life West, a region like a teenager, prone to the dramatic shock. The East is a calm middle-ager, with far fewer surprises. In Virginia the transitions are slow and subtle. Blue Ridge mountains fade to Piedmont hills which dissolve to the Tidewater plain that slopes to the sea.

We rolled eastward on a beeline highway across that flatland into Wakefield, a town that bills itself as the "Peanut Capital of the World," where the diner menu begins with peanut soup and ends with peanut pie. In antebellum days when this was plantation country the lowly ground pea was used for fattening hogs, but during the Civil War the peanut became so popular among soldiers on both sides that it has been this area's leading money crop ever since.

We were headed for the Blackwater River, and after a few more miles we turned onto a little blue byway that bisected some of those peanut fields. We put our canoes into the water under a bridge where the mud flat chronicled the traffic patterns of the local wildlife, which must congregate there like Times Square crowds on New Year's Eve, judging by the myriad bird and mammal tracks. Here the Blackwater is barely a notch above creek status—a stream that wiggles down through the scrub woods and truck farms of Virginia's southeastern corner, a pleasant but altogether ordinary diorama.

We had paddled a prosaic mile or so when suddenly our ordinary, familiar world vanished and we found ourselves in an exotic new one— so lush, so verdant, so fecund, so noisy, so alive, it was as if we had drifted into a tropical jungle. This was the Blackwater Swamp, not the legendary morass of gloom and doom, but a swamp so bright and cheerful it dispelled all the traditional negative connotations.

Floating into this mystical, magical liquid-and-light realm was like stepping into one of Monet's summer gardens, all dappled and shimmering surfaces. Instead of a foreboding darkness, there was a curious luminosity stage-lit with special effects. Sunbeams streamed like spotlights through openings in the canopy, then rebounded from the water to dance on tree trunks, quivering on the bark like the dazzling glints from a dance hall's mirrored ball.

Summer might have settled in just outside this terrarium, but inside we found the apogee of spring, an explosion of buds and birds. The branches were laden with dripping vines, the tree trunks decorated with dangling epiphytes, the canopy raucous with tiny songsters. A cheerful celebration was in progress, a joyous cacophony, like strings and woodwinds tuning up before a concert. We were surrounded by tumultuous sounds—owls' hoots, hawks' cries, warblers' arias, tree frogs' chants—what Turgenev called the "happy, laughing tremolo of spring."

bald cypress swamp

The only darkness was below, where the Blackwater now matched its name. It was no longer a river as we know it, but a mysterious flow through a watery forest on a flooded plain. The current running through it was invisible—no discernible flow or direction, no stream boundaries to contain and guide its course—inscrutable and a bit disconcerting in an engaging way.

The name Blackwater is only partially accurate. Seen from a canoe, the water is dark—a polished ebony—but scooped up in a cup it is actually a rich cognac. Tannic acid gives all of Virginia's southeastern swamp waters their dark color and also keeps the water fresh—so fresh, in fact, that eighteenth-century sailors prized the water from the nearby Great Dismal Swamp because it never went bad even on the longest voyages.

Huge silent sentries stood throughout this obsidian lake. The fabled bald cypresses, centuries-old giants with titanic trunks, have grown to miraculous heights, their crowns a green vault, their anchors hidden in the depths. Those giant trunks were mirrored in the black surface, and like a hall of mirrors, extended in a seemingly endless doubled progression of columns in all directions.

We floated along on this mirror, suspended between earth and sky, trees above and below as well, and in the absence of solid ground, somewhat disoriented, but again in an intriguing way, as reality and reflection merged in mystery. From a jet, the Blackwater must look like a thin linear strip of woods bisecting farm fields, yet within, there was the expansive feeling of a vast world separate from ordinary confines. I felt as if we could float on and on among those columns—yet I also felt enclosed, as if contained within a dewdrop world.

I'd been lured on this trip by the chance to see this unique world with Gary Williamson, who has been exploring bald-cypress tracts for decades and was brimming over with swamp lore. The wiry, wind- and sun-creased, boyishly enthusiastic Mark-Trail-straight-arrow naturalist now prowls coastal marshes as the ranger at False Cape State Park but returns to the Blackwater whenever he has a good excuse.

As a bonus, he had scheduled this trip during the spring warbler migration, and the Blackwater was a prime stopover for one of the best and the brightest—the gold-breasted, copen-winged prothonotary. Soon after we entered the swamp Gary identified the ubiquitous liquid lilting "sweet, sweet . . . sweet" as that warbler's call, and I scoured the canopy for an hour hoping for a glimpse of one of those elusive teases always flitting and calling just out of sight. Finally one took pity on me and cooperated, posing nearby on a low branch, breathtaking in a shaft of sunlight, performing with such joyous abandon that I wondered if it was singing, as avian experts say, to call a mate or claim a tree—or for the pure joy of reaching the promised land after its long journey from South America.

The woods were alive with the sound of all sorts of birdcalls. I recognized some lyrics—the Carolina wren's "teakettle," the towhee's "drink your tea," the pileated's Woody Woodpecker laugh—and was able to follow the sound to the songster. There were some that were hard to spot, like the "cigars with wings"—Gary's term for the chimney swifts that zoomed high above like F-14s—and some I couldn't miss, like the great blue heron.

The great blue is a stupendous bird, the Boeing 747 of the swamp, four feet tall with a six-foot wingspan. We watched a trio lift from the water, their wing flaps supple as Swan Lake ballerinas. They flew to the top of a nearby tree and landed with guttural squawks in a Kennedy-compound cluster of nests. (Herons must believe it takes a village.) Their nest construction surprised me. It was most unprofessional looking, freeform and flimsy, habitats that would never rate a feature in *Architectural Digest,* piles of sticks stacked so haphazardly and precariously that I wondered about the attrition rate for baby herons.

I also wondered how many birds I would have seen on a walk through my Blue Ridge mountain woods. On a typical morning I might see about a dozen species, but in this swamp, thanks to Gary's sharp eyes and expert ear, we spotted almost four dozen.

The plant life was just as amazing. Many trees actually thrive in this standing water—overcup oak, water tupelo, water hickory, even red maple—but it's the statuesque bald cypresses—the behemoths that Gary calls the "giant redwoods of the Southeast"—that outgrow and outlast the others.

Most of the Blackwater cypresses are three times as old as this country—already mature adults when the first Europeans arrived—and some are more than a thousand years old. Like their West Coast kin—the redwood and the sequoia—the cypresses indeed stand "like the Druids of old." Good genes help. The cypress resists fire and lightning and withstands hurricane-force winds, and like another pa-

triarch, the bristlecone pine, survives despite the loss of most of its
limbs.

Gary talked of state-champion trees the way breeders talk of best-
in-show dogs. Ratings are determined by a point system that involves
height, girth, and the spread of the crown, and by these criteria the
bald cypress is the largest tree east of the Rockies. The Blackwater is
the home of Virginia's state champ. We saw this titlist—with its thirty-
three-foot girth—and its neighbors, proud runners-up with crowns
fifteen stories high and trunks so huge that four of us could not have
joined hands and reached all the way around.

Those elder statesmen were rather remote but the latest generation was cropping up on old logs, offering an easy tip-to-root inspection. The cypress needles were a fresh spring green with a tinge of
neon lime, the branches more like feathers than evergreens. Because
of those needles, I was surprised to learn that the cypress is a deciduous in disguise. Its needles are "leaves" which turn rust and drop in
the fall—the reason for the "bald" in its name.

By midlife the cypress is both massive and delicate, those lacy
needles a distant green filigree high atop a mighty trunk whose soft
auburn bark has matured to a smooth and serious gray. Its base flares
to form a buttress, often tripling its width just above the water line.
And in the water surrounding the base, like moons around Jupiter, are
curious root projections called "knees," which proliferate with age, so
that an elderly monarch might have more than a hundred subjects at
its feet. These slippery stalagmites range from a few inches to eight
feet and more, some with cavelike openings big enough to conceal a
boater. Their function is still somewhat of a mystery, although many
experts think they aerate the root system.

The swamp has more moderate temperatures than its surroundings—like a cave, Gary told us, warmer in winter and cooler in summer. It's a haven for all seasons, perhaps the reason why the Blackwater is the northernmost limit of several species I'd never seen before,
Southerners such as the water tupelo and the cross vine.

That cross vine was my favorite new-to-me plant, intense red and yellow, a flamboyant Southern belle with luscious lips. The resurrection fern was a close second, partly because its name is so apt. It plays dead, a sere and brown cascade on a cypress trunk until a rejuvenating rain brings it back to startling verdancy.

The word "swamp" conjures visions of jungly vines, and the Blackwater has some striking ones—some as round as a logger's forearm and some as fine as a baby's tendril. Gary pointed out some individual climbing techniques: the cross vine makes a beeline for the tree crown, and the supplejack—"a strangler and a twister"—wraps itself snake-style around the massive columns. Everywhere was Moore's "deadly vine" that "doth . . . steep the flesh with blistering dew." Anyone who was unfamiliar with poison ivy might find this swamp dweller the most appealing, its white flower clusters dripping from creepers scrolled as gracefully as Arabic lettering.

Fallen cypress logs are often the only solid dry "land" around, and sometimes serve as revealing repositories of recent history. Two such logs were littered with the molluscan remnants of a raccoon dinner party. Emptied mussel shells lined the long table, and judging by all the broken crockery, it must have been quite a feast. I could just imagine the previous night's scene—like a *Wind in the Willows* banquet depicted by Arthur Rackham. The next log displayed the aftermath—rows of raccoon scat filled with tiny shell bits, evidence as unmistakable as pit-filled bear scat beneath a cherry tree.

Gary also found evidence of another furry swamp inhabitant. He cruised by another log, picked up a stick, and showed us the beaver tooth marks. The scars were neat and methodical, like those on a pencil chewed by a compulsive schoolboy. It was so interesting to see this minuscule evidence of beaver jaws after years of just spotting the big stuff—those pointed stumps that mark a beaver family's lumber camp.

The smaller logs might have been the tables and privies of the raccoons, but the fallen giants—in various stages of what swamp

observer Charles Stansbury called the "changeful verdure of decay"—
formed linear islands, fecund nurseries for the next generations of
elm, ash, and maple. Amidst these seedlings, bright gardens had
sprouted in the rich rot—clusters of papal purple violets and colo-
nies of circus-colored fungi.

Gary's practiced eye spotted life in the vegetation on these
islands, and he caught a khaki-camouflaged toad and a bright
lacquer-green tree frog for our close inspection. Judging by appear-
ances, frogs are the more alert of the two. The toad had a heavy-
lidded look, like a squat newly awakened Rip Van Winkle. The frog,
however, looked like an amphetamine junkie. I held it in my palm—
it was about two inches long, its black eyes wide, its little chest
heaving like that of a pulp romance heroine. It must have had stage
fright, because all around me other chorus members were boister-
ously chanting their mating refrain. This little frog might have been
capable of surprising sound—in many cases, the smaller the lungs,
the louder the voice.

There was one form of life I hoped we wouldn't encounter. I don't
share Indiana Jones's emotional aversion to snakes, and think of most
as lithe and wondrous beauties, to be studied in detail whenever I can
spot them. But I could envision a cottonmouth slowly uncoiling as we
drifted beneath its perch on a branch. Harmless brown snakes do
bask on branches, and Gary had seen more than thirty on a day's trip,
so it wasn't much of a stretch to think that a darker, venomous version might be poised to drop into our canoe.

Pit vipers aside, the Blackwater is the opposite of the stereotypical
dank and dour, fearsome and forbidding swamp. But it does deserve
one traditional appellation. It is mysterious—but in a way that kindles
not terror and flight but wonder and awe. It is a world apart, insulated from harsh winds and searing sun, with a moderation that en-
genders a sense of peace and serenity, a balance between things happening and things staying the same, between the tumultuous spring,
young and vibrant, exploding with sound and growth, and the bald

cypress, stately and ancient, timeless and tranquil, existing for centuries in Thoreau's "perennial waveless serenity."

As I floated among the massive trunks it was as if I were back in the cathedral at Chartres, standing amid the huge pillars beneath that granite vault, sunbeams streaming in through the rich reds of a stained-glass window. Again I was among giant columns, only this time beneath a lacy vault, sunbeams streaming in through the blues and greens of a natural Tiffany.

To be in such a place is to feel a visceral, emotional link to centuries past, and to make a physical connection as well. I touched those trees that were here before Columbus, and Longfellow's words—"This is the forest primeval"—came again to my mind, words that are as apt for these Methuselahs as they were for his "murmuring pines and hemlocks."

I also began to feel a primal connection with epochs past. The Blackwater has a strange prehistoric aura, like a timeless place that spans millennia back to the Jurassic age. I could almost imagine a pterodactyl swooping down from the canopy, a brontosaurus rising from the depths. In fact, a drawing of the Mesozoic era pterodactyl in flight resembles one of today's residents—the pileated woodpecker. And in that primordial setting it wasn't hard to believe that the ivory-billed woodpecker, a species that hasn't been seen for decades, might not be extinct after all but still alive in there somewhere, cavorting with its cockaded cousins.

The Blackwater's bald cypresses have been here long enough to help solve one of this country's most enduring mysteries—the disappearance of the Lost Colony. That first New World English settlement was on Roanoke Island just south of the Virginia line in what is now North Carolina, and its inhabitants vanished, leaving just one tantalizing clue—the word "Croatoan" carved on a tree near their abandoned fort.

Now that researchers are able to extract core samples from tree trunks, they can read the growth rings like a history book. They can see a "climate record" in the fluctuating patterns, with droughts marked by small spaces between the yearly rings. Few trees are old enough to reveal significant information, but the Blackwater's cypress elders were silent witnesses in the case of the missing settlers.

According to the cypress cores an epic dry spell—the worst three-year drought in eight hundred years—coincided with the 1587 settlement of Roanoke Island. The Lost Colony was the first—and perhaps the worst—"disaster area" in U.S. history, and now many historians think the colonists must have died of mass starvation.

Most of the early settlers who followed thought Virginia's wetlands were wastelands—"too wet to plow, too dry to fish"—and believed that the only good swamp was a drained swamp. They set about converting much of Virginia's swampy bottomlands into land suitable for agriculture. And if you couldn't drain 'em, steer clear of 'em, they said.

The undeserved but abiding reputation of this region was advanced by Colonel William Byrd after he led a 1728 expedition into the Blackwater's larger neighbor to the east. He said it was "dreadful" and "dirty" with air so foul that "not even a turkey buzzard will venture to fly over it," so foul that it kills most people and leaves the rest "no better than ghosts." Byrd's appellation—"The Great Dismal Swamp"—endured, and the libel continued with subsequent explorers describing the swampy regions as dank and dark lairs of snakes and spooks, marauders and moonshiners. A later sojourner, John Boyle O'Reilly, found the swamp to be "an agony of perverted nature . . . a vast and frightful phantasmagoria infested with repulsive and deadly creatures."

George Washington, on the other hand, surveyed the Great Dismal and proclaimed it a "glorious paradise." Finally, more than a century later, another supporter surfaced. An accurate assessment was issued by Charles Stansbury, a London journalist who came to the United States in 1874, explored the Great Dismal, and declared it a "veritable fairyland, a perfect setting . . . for a Midsummer Night's Dream."

My sentiments exactly. With its lush woods and dark waters, the Blackwater, like the neighboring Great Dismal, is a hidden jewel—an emerald set in obsidian—tucked away in an unassuming setting in the Tidewater flatlands.

A friend once took me to a dazzling spot on Georgian Bay in Ontario, a place so special that I understood at once why I had been sworn to secrecy as the condition for inclusion on the trip. It was the Isle of Capri on a North Woods shoreline. If I had stumbled upon the Blackwater swamp I might have kept its secret, revealing its location to only a handful of trusted friends. But someone far more generous of spirit than I found this enclave long ago and preserved it for the public, so those willing to set aside their notions of "swamp" could see this spot for themselves.

Back in the 1930s, John Russell Kirk bought a large tract of land in Southampton County to ensure a good supply of timber for his lumber mill. Despite the fact that "baldy cypress" was in great demand, he decreed the best and the biggest off-limits to his loggers. He thought these ancient trees were too venerable to be disturbed, and because of his instincts, we now have, according to dendrochronologist David W. Stahle, a tract that is "one of the best old-growth cypress forests left on this earth."

Kirk's conservation was all the more remarkable because of the value of these trees. Called "the wood eternal," cypress is so highly resistant to rot and decay that it has been used for everything from boats and bridges to grave markers and water pipes. In fact, hollow cypress logs installed as water pipes in New Orleans in 1798 were still intact when removed more than a century later.

Kirk's son, retired orthopedic surgeon Arthur Kirk, donated seventy-seven acres of this pristine tidewater forest to The Nature Conservancy in 1994. And a good thing he did, too. Most of our giants of the earth are gone. Of all the virgin timber in the "lower forty-eight," less than ten percent is still standing and much of that is threatened. Our swamps are vanishing as well. Developers have filled in more than half of our original wetlands.

It was "the primeval forests undefaced by the hand of man" that left a deep impression on Charles Darwin after his voyage around the world. "They bear the stamp of having lasted, as they are now, for ages, and there appears no limit to their duration through future time."

But he expressed that confidence before the days of pollution and desecration. So much of our wild solitude is threatened by those whose concept of recreation involves motors that leave noise, oil, grit, and tracks in their wake. Luckily, the boys who like speed-and-sound toys won't like this playground. No ground solid enough for their off-road vehicles, no channel deep enough for their speedboat propellers. So the swamp is safe from the sort of ATV recreator-desecrators who are trampling our fragile deserts and fouling our wild lakes.

But what of the pollutants, the silent, insidious threats sifting down from the sky, floating down from the farms? The bald cypress didn't fall to the axe or chain saw, but will it succumb to poisons?

To the west, Blue Ridge hemlocks are dying at a rapid rate. They withstood the woolly adelgid pest for decades, but now their days are numbered, in large part, botanists say, because they are weakened by air pollution and now lack the strength to survive. Skeletons of the first casualties stand as mute and stark premonitions of what the future might hold for their arboreal brethren. Other mountain species with crippled constitutions are now on life support, vulnerable to insect predators. Could air pollution fatally weaken the cypress as well?

And what of the water in the swamp? A river runs through it. And what else? Hog wastes? Lethal acids? Heavy metals? Copper, for instance, added to animal feed to prevent spoilage, is leaching from factory farms and scientists are finding high levels in river sediments.

The Nature Conservancy can't enclose the Blackwater in a protective bubble, so the swamp is vulnerable to toxins from faraway smokestacks and nearby hog farms. Wendell Berry urged us to "Invest in the millennium. Plant sequoias." Adapted for the Blackwater, the motto would be "Invest in the millennium. Save cypresses."

A virgin forest is a wilderness in the most complex and complete sense of that word, and as Aldo Leopold warned, "wilderness is a resource which can shrink but not grow." The Blackwater Preserve cannot be recreated; it cannot be cloned. We need to protect not only this precious patch, but the air and water that journey here from afar.

The Blackwater River Preserve—like Virginia's barrier islands—isn't on many vacationers' "must-see" lists. It's not paved, parking-lotted, snack-barred, water-slided. There's no billboard advertising the "closest motel to the swamp." The state's "for lovers" campaign lures tourists with visions of historic homes, Atlantic beaches, and storied Shenandoah. Visitors don't hear much about this swampland preserve—our emerald in the rough.

But I want to seize people by the lapels and say, "Come with me, just look at this! This place is amazing!"

I'll be back here soon. I'll return in summer to escape the torridity, when the swamp offers a climate far cooler than the sizzling surroundings. And in autumn to catch the colors, when the mirrored surface offers a double dose of saffron and cinnabar.

And perhaps I'll return if I need regeneration. There's a good case history to support a swamp-cure theory. Robert Frost once journeyed to the nearby Great Dismal, reportedly intending to end his life there after a woman rejected not only his book of poems but also his affections. But the swamp so revived his spirits and restored his optimism that he was able to return home and win the hand of that fair lady editor, Elinor White.

Writer Noel Mostert said that entering the Sahara was "like passing into a vast chamber that earth has surreptitiously held in trust." He could have said the same on entering the Blackwater. Its lush woods and dark waters, its rich profusion and stately order are surreptitiously tucked away in its unassuming Tidewater setting. The earth—and John Russell Kirk—have held this swamp in trust for us. Let us keep that trust.

Ellen Dudley is the author (with Eric Seaborg) of *American Discoveries,* winner of the Barbara Savage "Miles From Nowhere" Award. She is the author of *The Savvy Adventure Traveler* and the co-author (with Seaborg) of *Hiking and Backpacking.* Her work has appeared in newspapers including the *Rocky Mountain News,* the *Cleveland Plain Dealer,* and the *Seattle Times.* She is working on a book about Blue Ridge wildlife— flora and fauna and human—as seen from her vantage point on the Shenandoah National Park border.

Blackwater River Preserve was established in 1994 by Arthur and Marie Kirk's donation of seventy-seven acres to The Nature Conservancy.

Fist-Cloud at Laurel Fork
Laurel Fork

Jack Wennerstrom

Fat summer clouds swell with facets of light and curl their gilded edges, drag their scrolls off the ridges or down the knotted valleys. There is perfume of pitch and cow dung. Blue spikes of bugloss line roadways bent like hobbles, roses swallow wooden gates in pink and fuchsia gulps, and daylilies clot the veins of ditches or sag beside split-rail fences. Here and there, out past the bumpy streams and positioned below hazed ridges so vast and green that they miniaturize man's landscapes, rise comic Jack-and-Jill hilltops, barren as goose bumps or necklaced by sheep and cedars, evoking an absurd false innocence. For this is a region of conflict eons old, of immense and staggering flux, of slow relentless battle. These valleys lost their innocence when the mighty Himalayas were but a tectonic gleam in the Earth's randy eye. The evidence of struggle lingers. The very sky suggests it as you cruise the curves south of Franklin, West Virginia, on your way toward Monterey. A great clenched fist of cumulus—a giant's gnarled mitt of vapor—now swings above a ridgetop, slow and sinuous, deceptively mighty, today as ever before.

This is Appalachian country: a part-African crustal mongrel, named by a European, settled by Asian-linked trees, and presently part of melting-pot North America. Hernando de Soto trod its southern toe in what we now call Alabama and named it for the Apalachee Indians of the Gulf Coast. But 570 million years before the Europeans, continental plates discovered America, fusing rock of African origin with that in place here, then folding and faulting and lifting the lot for another 300 million annual cycles, to heights higher than Everest. Erosion bore down between lengthy upliftings. It was 200 million years before the first land organisms showed up. But then they appeared in abundance, from the hickories, walnuts, and magnolias that arrived with the Asian land bridge, to fantastic creatures of the Pleistocene—the moose-high short-faced bear, stilt-legged walking eagle, bruin-sized giant beaver, mammoth, ground sloth, and saber-toothed cat—to the Holocene plethora of flowering plants: at least fifteen hundred species, more floral varieties than those of any like-sized area in temperate North America. By then it was a place called by tribesmen "the endless mountains," a place so fecund of woody plants that the Senecas worshiped its giant trees and based their own origins upon them.

This is also headwaters country. The very rains that fell of old and now threaten to tumble from this fist-cloud—the rains that together with wind and heat, cold and complex settlement, eroded this long train of peaks—still gather here to birth mighty streams like the James and the Potomac. Water was a crucial weapon in the atmosphere's war on these rocks. It's a battle of a half-billion years, still being played out around you.

And while elements clash with the earth, modern man fights with the facts here. Lord Fairfax, whose wealth was linked to the bend of rivers and the fount of their beginnings, fought with His Majesty's Council to prove that the river "Potowmack" issued from its northern reach. Later, the boundary rights of counties and states, contested for over a century, were likewise linked to this North Branch. But Virginians near Monterey dispute their own founding fathers, claiming the Potomac's "most distant fountain"—to use the Council's phrasing—must be in their present state, where the South Branch issues from a field "most distant" from the river's mouth.

If you come upon old Jacob Hevener, of Hightown in Highland County, he'll tell you they've stopped by for decades, writers and photographers from far-flung magazines and papers, to capture the seminal Potomac as it bubbles up from a water trough nestled just behind the barn.

"But that's not really the spot," he'll declare in his thoughtful drawl, this sixth-generation product of the first axe-wielding Heveners. "The South Branch starts up on that hill there. Comes down along that tree line. Just follow it up behind that house. Then again, it could be that branch further on that's actually longer. Follows that second tree line. Up into those hills. Fact is, not everyone agrees."

Thus do slow, quiet conflicts stretch on here.

northern flying squirrel on red spruce

Indeed Mr. Hevener's valley, the "Blue Grass Valley" he calls it, is just one more line of battle, the Battle of the Half-Billion Years. But who would ever guess? It's as peaceful and lovely as any place on earth. It is morning, and you follow Route 640, up toward Blue Grass itself, a town so tiny it is bullied by mists, which threaten to swallow it whole. Meadowlarks and bluebirds carol or coast from the roadside wires, and there are those Mother Goose hillbumps again, this time sprinkled with idle beeves, shrunk to knickknack size by the slopes of Lantz Mountain and aswim now and then in the dark mobile ponds of cloud-shadows poured from the heights.

You turn west and follow the gravel. Higher and higher still. The road
crews are out. Fighting the mountain and the elements both, to keep each
from claiming their turf. Your world is a switchback world: to go forward
you retreat, with perfect switchback logic. If it weren't for a place called
Laurel Fork you would leave the Ridge and Valley realm and collide with
that gateway to the Dan'l Boone West: the Allegheny Front. Somewhere
past four thousand feet you would crash the Eastern Divide: streams on
one side reach Atlantic shores; on the other they flow to the Gulf. The
Potomac drainage will hold you instead, with its sharp-veined dendritic
creeks, pulsing north and east. Perhaps its "most distant fountain" is
really somewhere below, where Laurel Fork's rackety springs swell up to
the south and west? But that wouldn't end the conflict. Not in these strife-
needy hills, whose very beauty is forged by a fight, whose weapons in the
war of time and life are shaped by every struggle.

No matter. There is Laurel Fork now, jewel of the Alleghenies, purl-
ing over a mossy ledge and slip-stepping under a bridge. The sandstone
banks above it are hung with the very woody plant from which it draws
its name. Rosebay rhododendron, called "laurel" by hill-country natives, is now in perfect bloom, its white to pink massed flowers slung
from each gloss-leaved branchlet in candelabra clusters. Here it graces a
stony ledge, there a dense green alcove, and where it has found a streamside grip, stoops almost to the shining flow. Cherry, maple, ash, beech,
with black and yellow birch, are the bulk of its hardwood neighbors.
But now the pitch scent thickens, for here the hardwoods do battle with
their ancient subalpine foes, the spruces and the hemlocks.

Today debate still simmers as to who won the battles of old and
who—conifer or broadleaf—is winning them today. A warming trend
in the interglacial past once favored the deciduous phalanx; the return
of cold brought the softwood lines back—but when, for how long,
exactly where, and for what other reasons than climate? Complex theories abound. Choose your own from the many, as the first trees chose
their weapons. Were wide leaves best, to catch more summer rays and
convert more food for storage? What if spring was late, fall early, and

the frost so deep you went thirsty? Was it better to forge needle leaves, waxy and tough against wind and frost, against salvos of ice and snow? Better to be shallow rooted in the thin and rocky soils, where water runs off with such speed? Better to keep leaves year-round, in this place of chance nutrition, than to squander your strength on re-growth? It was not really up to them, of course. Time and troposphere told. The cloud-fist and his cohorts have the last word on these slopes.

"Northern Hardwood Forest" is what some call these Laurel Fork highlands. It suggests that the broadleafs have won. "Transition Forest" is a better term. In its strictest sense it describes that tier of woodlands that fence the mixed deciduous trees from the boreal softwoods of the north. Here, especially, it defines a zone of flux. Groves of red spruce and hemlock invade these deciduous slopes, overrun stream bends or high meadow edges, and, as nowhere else in Virginia, occur as scattered pickets among the hardwood ranks. "Transition" implies that the battle is in doubt, and that, indeed, is the case.

A Canadian esprit fills these southern woods. You could say that a ribbon of Canada droops down the Appalachians. For when glaciers at last pulled north, they left in place biota well adapted to the rigors of cold. And these high ridgetops sustained that cold as no place east or west. Thus, if you wend up toward Bear Wallow Run and follow the Laurel Fork feeders, you'll find holdouts of Canada mayflower, its fragrant white racemes and cleft, heart-shaped leaves more a fixture of Labrador summers. *Millium effusum*, or tall oat grass, is at home in Nova Scotia, but here it nods in the rocky woods. White baneberry, wood sorrel, bluebead lily, bog goldenrod, round-leaved orchis—these and more occur here, yet would equally fit a botanical list for Ontario or Quebec. Vertebrates known by our neighbors to the north are also well represented, especially breeding birds. Winter wrens, sapsuckers, grouse, saw-whet owls and Swainson's thrushes, magnolia and mourning warblers, swamp and vesper sparrows, juncos, creepers, kinglets, and nuthatches—the list is long of Laurel Fork birds nesting south of their prime northern range. Mammals of the frost show up here, too, like fishers and snowshoe hares, or the northern flying squirrel and secretive water shrew. Some species are boreal remnants, others disjuncts of the nearby Plateau, while a few—like twin-leaf toothwort, halberd-leaf violet, spring beauty—grace regions to the south or east, disappear in between, then recur in these highlands. And some twenty-five species at Laurel Fork exist nowhere else in Virginia.

Which has led to another battle. What is loosely referred to as Laurel Fork is a ten-thousand-acre preserve—a Special Management Area—owned for three-quarters of a century by the U.S. Forest Service. And leased by them as well. Leased, to the horror of protectionists long enamored of Laurel Fork's treasures, to companies like Thornwood Gas. The utility's permit, approved in 1996, to build a pipeline along Laurel Fork's flanks, hinted to several watchdog groups that drilling might soon follow. Hackles rose. But with The Nature Conservancy as referee, six environmental groups who had mustered behind SELC (Southern Environmental Law Center) to head off the threat of drilling compromised with Thornwood Gas, agreeing to allow the pipeline if Thornwood would cede its drilling rights to none other than The Nature Conservancy. Thus broader conflict was averted.

But, as one Thornwood spokesman observed, "environmentalists value the surface," while utilities covet deep earth. Here, on this age-old battlefield of rock, it seems but a matter of time before skirmish lines re-form.

One small piece of Laurel Fork the gasworks may never get. If you drift down from Bear Wallow Run to the junction of three different roads, you close on this parcel of paradise. A wild turkey hen appears in your path, bobs and zigzags roadrunner-style to the sheltering margin of green. You park at a gate and stretch your legs, listen to a tapping like men with tools, signaling back and forth by knocking on hollow posts. This is *Sphyrapicus varius*, the yellow-bellied sapsucker, breeding here at the bottom of its range and drumming this way with its beak. Theories as to why are many: food search, ritual courtship, boundary defense and bonding, even a thing called displacement, where frustrated birds have been known to charge shrubs, beat up convenient branches, even set upon harmless neighbors. These today hardly worry you; it sounds like a pair reinforcing their bond, a mutual exchange of endearments.

The air smells of ferns and rotted wood, of resins, fungi, dampness. The land before you is Goodall land, in the Goodall clan since the 1940s. You poke around by the entrance road, lifting rocks blackbear fashion, hoping for a glimpse of that rare hilltop herp, the Cheat Mountain salamander. In this land of lungless salamanders—West Virginia alone sports twenty-one species—who breathe instead through the pores in their skin, several types claim minute ranges. The Shenandoah salamander *(Plethodon n. shenandoah)* holds talus slopes of a few high hills only several square miles in size; its cousin *(Plethodon n. hubrichti)* prowls the wet woods at Peaks of Otter, a pair of humps in the Blue Ridge. Next to them these Cheat Mountain brethren are virtual hogs for property, roaming several counties in the state of West Virginia. And, of course, some acres at Laurel Fork. They look like their relatives the red-backs, and indeed you find a red-backed when turning a slab of stone. But Cheat Mountain bellies are black, not light; this one instantly fails the test. You return it to its secret spot and reflect on its vertical living space, for woodland species climb and descend in the loamy layers of their turfs. Some claim that in prime Appalachian locations the earth below just one acre may hold two and one-half million red-backs. You dismiss this figure from your mind. It is simply too startling to accept.

You are up now, prowling for rarer finds. When along comes Ches Goodall in his truck. Forester scion of a forest conservationist. Has Laurel Fork in his blood. Verner Daniel arrives as well, land protection specialist for Virginia's chapter of The Nature Conservancy, which owns a pretty parcel here of nearly four hundred acres. We'll take a hike together, get aired out on the ridges.

Down then, from the lumber road. Across Laurel Fork on a hanging limb, sinking into the sedges. Grassy beds of the narrow-gauge tracks that log trains once used to get up here are humped beneath our feet. Three or four *Lycopodiums*—those ancient plants most call club-moss—all growing within stride's length. Thick mats of sphag-num—their living tips tinged like Victorian brocade to shades of maroon and puce—carpet the spongy spring banks or blot some rooty ledge. Tanagers call, and pewees. Sunlight sifts the gloom. Wood- and hay-scented ferns lace the runes of their old green symmetry above the forest floor, like clues to the riddle of beauty.

But the mood is one of travel and pace and you don't really halt for long. Ches is anxious to show you the best, each spot that inspires his stewardship. The day has gotten warm. Cuckoo spit shines in the meadows—that white foamy clot of the spittlebug nymph, designed to conceal its frailty.

Design, in fact, is the name of the game. Design forged by grace under pressure, fitted by time for the fight. The fisher's black eye gleams for battle, not beauty. Its keenness, the very roundness and set of its clear liquid gaze, its honed binocular perception, is for sifting squirrels or partridge chicks out of the maze of a pine woods. Like-wise its nose and ears. The length of its fur carries meaning and weight, the thickness of each hair, the curve of every claw, down to the last pulse of whisker. These are the weapons that time beats out, whets from trial and death. The fact that perfect tools have also the prettiest taper or tone, shimmer, sheen, or shape, is not a happy accident but the litmus test for life.

A deer now bounds ahead. And Ches has found some boletes, those lurid gill-less mushrooms, velvet to the touch, that perform so well in the pot. Is flavor a function of form? Perhaps deep in the recess of the brain.

Up and around toward the Hannah Tract, eyeing what looks like bear scat, catching the flute of a veery—or is it a hermit thrush? Old man White cleared his homestead here, hunkered in the lee of this cove. Now all that's left is the red-spruce break that he planted up above, just northwest of the homestead.

And a fine little heath bald it is. Scooped out between two hills— The Saddle, in fact, is its moniker—it bristles with low-bush blueberry. Thick as springs on a mattress. A beaver traversing would bounce. And maybe even a black bear, if it weren't too busy eating. Bounce on a bed of berries. An ericaceous trampoline to tempt all those who pass.

And, as Verner and Ches both point out, its countenance suggests the West. Montana or Wyoming. Perhaps some foothills in the Wind River range, with its dark green corona of spruce spires, its meadow inviting Griz.

A hawk calls from a spruce snag; Verner echoes it neatly—"keeer-r-r!" he cries to the red-tailed—and picks a palmful of berries, grinning. You pick and grin as well, and watch as you do the cloud-fist in the blue above the meadow—really just a thumb today, and half a hazy finger. Ches strips his berries with expert speed, then leads us over to a red-spruce grove, where young trees unfurling their fresh new growth—delicate needles of palest green—stand patient below their seniors, stalling for their chance. They require this protection from above as they wait for a frost kill or windfall to cut them a key to the sun. Alone, their future is dim.

Indeed, this need for a canopy of elders among the spruce and fir provides one of the theories for why balds are here. Interglacial heat killed the middling-altitude spruces, hardwoods slowly replaced them, then cold of the present epoch beat the hardwoods back. But without any bigger buddies the spruce could not reseed in the bare zones left by the broadleafs. Thus grasses, or the tough-stemmed *Ericaceae*—those laurels, azaleas, blueberries, and such of the family known as heaths—filled these marginal niches. There's a lot of fine-tuning to this theory, and it's joined by at least six others: that nomads cleared or burned these spots to encourage mountain oat grass, or to fashion sacred sites; that settlers cleared them for cattle; that insects or native ruminants gradually ground them down; that pockets of ice, wind, or drought reduced them long ago; that they only occur at the tolerance limit of the dominant species of tree; and finally, that each bald is unique and springs from distinctive causes. No one quite agrees, and feuds among factions are legion.

Sapling Ridge is next. You pass a little peat-dark pond full of pollywogs and newts and edged by frigid springs, squeeze through a split-rail fence, stride toward four thousand feet. Sweat soaks your shirt in the sunshine; you are puffing like a steam train, breathless when you reach the top. But here is a view worth sweating for: Spruce Knob asteam in the distant haze, Dolly Sods past that, the slopes and peaks in an arc so wide it makes you feel like a spittlebug nymph, helpless and small, wrapped in your damp weave of cotton. High meadows drop to the trees whose tops are now below you, pitch breezes dry your T-shirt, a wild turkey struts the ridge spine. The fist-cloud here adds a finger that it clenches against the sky.

Down again. Into a grove of hemlock and spruce that has the feel of old growth. A wee cathedral of calm, you on your back with the spires above, arrowed at the heavens. A redstart twitters, and a golden-crowned kinglet. You rise and stroke the furrowed bark—like the hide on some mammoth's leg, some motionless giant of columnar lines dredged up from the fiction of the past. You pace off one fallen hero—a hemlock of dusky hue—and it tops a hundred feet, like most of its still-standing mates.

Double-time back to the truck. Laurel bursting on the hillsides, wood sorrel matted through the woods. Lunch beckons. And what a lunch it turns out to be—consumed in an antique rocker on the broad porch of a cabin that overlooks a pier-glass pond and a scrim of shaggy spruces. And Ches's mother, Wayne—still the belle of Sweet Briar College—is there to complete the welcome, offering a tour of this lovely log house that seems conjured from the pages of a book. All the perks of a ridge runner's life with almost none of the pitfalls. Not just beauty at your doorstep, but beauty behind it as well.

You see now why there was such a fuss, such readiness for battle. You would no more wish Laurel Fork drilled and piped than the Sistine Chapel gutted. And the stock of your two companions has managed to soar as well. Strong men. Smart men. Determined men. Good men in a fight.

That's what it always gets down to, it seems, in these age-old southern mountains. A battle is never far off. It is futile to fight the mountains, of course, or try to topple the fist-cloud. But if man is his own worst enemy here, how do you save him from himself? What weapon has time evolved that counters the foe within?

Maybe one exists. Maybe you saw it on the mountain. Saw it when Ches eyed that fat bolete or that fleeing white-tailed deer. Heard it in Verner's hawk cry. Tasted it at The Saddle, when all of you stripped those berries as if they were bloody pearls, then gulped them like giddy boys. Felt it on Sapling Ridge, or beside that peat-dark pond, or flat on your back in the old growth, when the world turned upside down. Yes, surely that was it. Linked to design and detail again, to the scales on a moth or spruce cone, the speckles on a mountain trout. To those woven fragments of function and form that have conquered down the years. A thing so ephemeral, a weapon so fine-honed and fleeting in the shaping vapors of time that perhaps only human beings can claim it as their own. It goes by several names. Some just call it "spirit." Others, "joy" or "soul." It is what all children burst with, that force they cannot contain. Its power outstrips its size. Vastly. The glint of a salamander's ground tones, the twitch of a whitetail's ear. Tiny things, but they draw this genie from its bottle. And then you may see a weapon rise for the battles that lie ahead. A weapon as fine as the Laurel Fork mists but as potent as a giant's fist.

Jack Wennerstrom—writer, teacher, and lecturer—is the author of two books, *Soldiers Delight Journal* and *Leaning Sycamores*. He currently teaches nature writing at Loyola College and for BioTrek Naturalists, Inc. in Baltimore, Maryland.

The Nature Conservancy acquired the 374-acre Laurel Fork Preserve in 1990, and continues to work on land protection efforts in Virginia's "Red Spruce Highlands."

CHRISTMAS WITH EAGLES
Mason Neck

Judith Kahn

A Holi-day in Four Parts

Part One: Christmas with Eagles

Christmas morning. The gift of two eagles. Eyeing the waters of Belmont Bay. On a crystal day. The ground rimmed with ice and a dusting of frozen snow. Holly leaves and pine needles shimmering with the sun's natural tinsel. Two eagles atop two trees, watching for food, on Mason Neck.

Jutting out into the Potomac River, less than twenty miles from the nation's capital, the eight-thousand-acre boot of the Mason Neck peninsula is a haven for eagles. In the late 1960s, when DDT sent eagle populations plummeting and plans for development threatened to destroy the peninsula's intricate ecosystem, the first national wildlife refuge created specifically to protect the bald eagle was established at Mason Neck.

It was largely a grassroots effort, spearheaded by the indomitable Elizabeth Hartwell, who is probably drafting an action alert even as I write. For the task of saving wildness is never complete. It requires constant vigil, at Mason Neck, and around the globe. Even now development looms inevitable at the top of the Neck where two private landowners, each with very large tracts, are discussing the future of their holdings. But a single individual can make a difference. A single individual can save a species. A single individual, through unrelenting spirit, endless hours of impossible work, and sheer will, can save a habitat from the bulldozer.

When talk turned to changing this critical habitat into airstrips, a residential community of twenty thousand, a massive landfill, a thirty-six-inch gas pipeline, a commercial dredging project, a deep-sea marine terminal, a scientific and industrial exposition, an outer beltway with an eight-lane highway crossing the Potomac at Mason Neck, or countless other projects that threatened the peninsula in the 1960s and 1970s, Liz Hartwell went to work. She galvanized a community, creating a fate for Mason Neck greater than convenience or financial gain.

Liz mobilized the energies of concerned citizens, gained the attention of government and private agencies, and succeeded in saving Mason Neck, its wildlife, and all of us from irrevocable loss. In 1967, The Nature Conservancy first purchased land on Mason Neck, holding it in trust until government funds could be appropriated. The Conservancy continued land acquisitions into the 1970s, and now the federal government's Fish and Wildlife Service manages the 2,277-acre Mason Neck National Wildlife Refuge, and the Virginia Department of Conservation and Recreation oversees the 1,813-acre Mason Neck State Park. They are engaged in a cooperative effort to protect and preserve the nesting, roosting, and feeding habitats of the bald eagle and all of the wildlife that make Mason Neck their home.

Today, there are seven active eagle nests on the Mason Neck peninsula. They are located on the refuge, in the state park, on the grounds of the Gunston Hall Plantation, and on private residential property. The management of this delicate balance of wildlife and human habitation and recreation is a joint initiative at the national, state, and local levels, among government agencies and private citizens.

Last Christmas, 118 eagles were counted at Mason Neck. Their numbers fluctuate from year to year and from season to season. Numbers are highest in the early and midwinter when approximately forty to sixty individual birds can usually be seen in the lower portion of the boot. In addition to the resident population, eagles come down from farther north, attracted by the open and protected waters of the Potomac River system where foraging and roosting are favored. In the summer months, eagles come up from the south, though numbers are generally lower. This northward and southward movement makes Mason Neck a crucial roosting and feeding habitat, not only for resident eagles, but for the entire mid-Atlantic eagle population. Whole species of birds have disappeared from a specific region or gone extinct because they lost their wintering grounds or summer and breeding habitats.

Eagles are not the only beneficiaries of Liz Hartwell's efforts. In the protected forests, marshes, shoreline, and waters of the refuge and the park, otter, fox, and more than two hundred species of birds and waterfowl thrive throughout the year. Surrounded by Belmont and Occoquan Bay to the west, Pohick and Gunston Cove to the east, and the Potomac River to the south, tens of thousands of migrating buffleheads, mergansers, ruddy ducks, and countless other water birds find rest and sustenance during the arduous fall and spring migrations and in the winter months. Mason Neck also has the largest freshwater marsh in northern Virginia, with one of the most significant great blue heron rookeries in the mid-Atlantic region; there are close to twelve hundred nesting pairs.

An eagle has seven thousand feathers and an eight-foot wingspan. Powerful legs and sharp talons for seizing and pressing its victims, keen eyesight for spotting prey at great distances, impressive diving speeds, and a hooked beak for flesh eating make it one of the most formidable hunters in all of the animal kingdom.

I had seen my first eagle eighteen years ago in a marsh in Florida. A great dark bird was flying overhead, low in the sky, with yellow legs and a white tail and a white head. And a dark heavy body and big dark wings. I knew it was an eagle. Though I had never seen one. Except in Federal Express ads and photographs. It circled over my head, lower and lower in the sky. It flew to a nearby tree, one of only two in the marsh. It perched a moment on a low branch. Then flew to the other. Back and forth, from one tree to the other, each time, over my head. I fell to my knees. I took off my shoes. I looked up. It flew and perched and flew and circled and perched and circled and flew and flew, as though performing for this girl below. I was enraptored.

Then the eagle flew toward the forest. I followed, barefoot along the raised causeway, toward where the trees thickened in the wood. There I stopped. The bird was sitting in a tree. I saw the large white head. It turned and looked me in the eye. I raised my glass. The head filled the frame of my binoculars. I saw it eye to eye. This was no ordinary bird. This was no ordinary seeing. I was seeing it in close-up, eye to eye, as I knew it was seeing me. There was no distance between. All distance vanished by the power of its vision, far greater than the power of my field glasses. Of any eye on earth. I disappeared in its stare, devoured by the power of its sight.

It seemed to project something reserved for humans, but decidedly not human. An intelligence that was not mental. Consciousness without word or sentiment. Chilling. Singular. Illuminating. A wholeness that shattered and unified. And terrified.

The glass burst in my hand.

An eagle sees in ways we can not
comprehend, that transcend the borders of our senses. Like the rays of sun that burn our skin but do not give heat. Finer than the light of seeing. They pierce the unseen with a power that can see newsprint from one end zone to the other.

Now I know the higher concentration of visual cells and nerve fibers in the eyes of raptors are primarily responsible for this extraordinary vision. A hawk has about one million per square millimeter, compared to four hundred thousand in a sparrow, and two hundred thousand in the human eye. Moreover, the pecten, a comblike organ

in the back of their eyes which supplies blood, also throws shadows
on the retina, sharpening the perception of movement, which makes
it possible for an eagle to see a rabbit from the distance of a mile. In
addition, the muscles in the eyes of diurnal birds of prey are composed of striated fibers designed for extremely rapid changes of focus, unlike the smooth fibers in the eyes of mammals. This makes it
possible for them to shift focus in flight at extremely great speeds, in
dives approaching and exceeding one hundred miles an hour.

But then I only knew I was transfixed. Gone into the eye of the
eagle. I looked at the eyes and beak and face of this blinding creature
for no length of time. There was no length of time. No length. No
time. No measure. Only Being. Which, at any moment, at every moment, could tear my face apart.

And it looked at me.

To be looked at by a bald eagle is to be seen
and devoured,
is to be
transformed.

It is not for us to look at eagles. But for eagles to look at us.
And for us to be willing
to be
eaten.
Consumed
by this bird of prey, and so become the bird,
seeing as the eagle sees.

This is a mystery of birth and death and resurrection that an eagle
gave me one fine day in a marsh in Florida. I can't tell you how, nor
articulate the what. I can only relay the story. I had stumbled upon a
myth. Contained in the archetype of eagle. The myth of resurrection, of

the eternal return of the beginning; a beginning that starts with an end.

Some American Plains Indians believe birds share the religion of humans. Maybe because they are both two-legged. Maybe because birds seem closest to heaven, messengers of the Gods. On this fine Christmas Day, I believe it, too. They are my companions in spirit as I relive birth and death and resurrection, sharing religion with the great Bird of Prey. What finer way to spend Christmas Day than with eagles, the bearers of this story.

Each species has a story to tell. Each is a living text, part of the great Oral Tradition. Each has a gift to give to consciousness. Each *is* a gift of consciousness. And in the human species, that consciousness can be realized.

Our spiritual traditions teach us this. In Christianity the eagle heralds the messianic age, bringing new life and knowledge of God. The animals in their great archetypal forms inform the Gospels and the Hebrew Bible, also called the Torah. The Book of Job directs us to "ask the beasts and they shall teach thee, and the fowls of the air, and they shall tell thee." In the Talmud, the compilation of centuries of Jewish thought and one of the most influential and authoritative texts in all of Judaism, it says if we had not been given the Torah, we would have been able to learn its teachings from observing the behavior of different animals. In many Native American traditions, the vision quest is a physical journey in a natural environment seeking an encounter with the spirit-nature of a natural life form for guidance on one's path. Their Medicine Wheel is a template of the four directions, each represented by an animal, used to help chart the way through consciousness.

The creatures of the earth are sacred. They are eternal seeds, divine teachings. God instructed Noah to build an ark and fill it with the animals. Everything else could be swept away in the flood. But when we lose creatures we lose portions of Torah that can never be retrieved. With every life form that becomes extinct we lose a portion of the great body of oral teaching that will never again be told. The animal and plant kingdoms are indeed the living Word that can never be written down. Once they are gone, they are gone, and their wisdom is forever lost to the Earth and to human consciousness.

Soul needs plants and animals to grow and mature. The human spirit needs wilderness to evolve. Why was the first human task naming the animals? Why did the Children of Israel and the mixed multitudes wander in the wilderness for so many years, and there receive the Word of God? Soul feeds on wildness. While most of us can survive with trace amounts, those traces are critical. Even more critical to soul's timeless journey is the fact of its existence, the *possibility* of wildness, without which the human would cease to develop toward its highest manifestation. Imagine a world without the Eagle, the Tiger, the Gorilla, and the Whale? Indeed, it is that very imagination that would suffer in a world devoid of the great archetypal forms living in the wild. Our imaginations, our psyches, and our spirits would be radically diminished; and we, as a species, would not reach our fullest potential. Churches, synagogues, temples, mosques, these are important sanctuaries for the cultural community. But so also is the bird sanctuary and the wildlife refuge, the natural community, where humans also come to meet their God.

As the sun set on Belmont Bay in the clear chill of Christmas day, the barking of the tundra swans was conversational and close. In the lavender and mauve water reflecting air reflecting water, as river and sky became one, the swans' whiteness was magical, and the sound of their wings slapping the water as they took to the air in twos.
Good *Shabbos.*

Part Two: Shabbos in the Great Marsh

The next day was Saturday, Shabbos, the Jewish Sabbath. It began the night before, as the sun set into the bay, as the day in Jewish tradition begins at sundown.

I drove to the Great Marsh in the arch of the boot of Mason Neck, the very heart of the sole. Two hundred and fifty acres of water and grass, soothing to the eye and mind, food to the spirit. A critical area in the national wildlife refuge.

My Saturday sanctuary was often the bird sanctuary. Shabbos is time to return the world to its natural state. God commands us not to work, the kind of work that uses technical skill to convert the resources of the natural world for our own consumption. Shabbos is time to stop doing and start being. To stop creating in order to participate in creation. To set aside the tasks, ambitions, and preoccupations of the human mind, to connect with the animal soul, to access the Divine spirit.

I began my Shabbos ritual to get out of my thinking mind. The first law of Shabbos: No thinking. The only goal of Shabbos: No goal. Except to wander without preconception, assumption, or expectation. To help stop my mental chatter, I smoked to the six directions. I invoked the spirit of the East: illumination, vision, the color gold, the creature eagle. I faced South: nose to the ground, the spirit of wonder, trust, and innocence. The mouse. The color green. To the West I called on the great Black Bear: healing, introspection, curing fear. My creature of late. To the North: wisdom, the color white, and grace. Then up to Father Sky and down to Mother Earth, seeking guidance and protection from above, ease through matter from below, and headed for the trail.

The trail went through woods.

The woods went on for a long time.

Then I glimpsed it through the trees: the Great Marsh. I didn't know if my jaw dropped visibly or not. It was an awesome sight. I felt it in the front and back of my chest. A great opening and filling and relaxing. And in my shoulders and spine. I continued walking. I was learning this was a marsh at the end of trees. I had to walk through a forest to get there.

A man passed me on the trail from the other direction.

"There's an eagle off to the left," he said as he passed.

When I got to the marsh, my jaw did drop. There was no where else I wanted to be. I felt grateful and privileged to be there.

After a while, I looked through my binoculars. A lot of ducks were flying. I followed three of them with my field glasses. They seemed gray and black and mostly dark. Maybe brown. It was hard to make out color in the overcast sky. Then a flash of brilliant, iridescent blue, the speculum, that rectangular patch at the bottom of the wing when they dipped toward me in flight. Black ducks? Mallards? Black ducks. Maybe.

Suddenly there was a great commotion somewhere out in the marsh. A great chortling, whistling, honking, and barking was going on. I lowered my glasses. I looked out. It seemed to be coming from the white birds way out in the ponds.

In a marsh it is sound as much as seeing. True everywhere in wildness. Sound is meaning. In the written and spoken word. In woods and waters and cries of creatures, day and night. Look with your ears; listen with your eyes. See and hear as creatures do.

I looked at the white waterfowl through my field glasses. A marsh hawk flew into view. Marsh hawks are among my favorites. Maybe because they fly low and are easy to see and watch for a long time. Maybe because of their amber feathers or white rump patch or beautiful barred wings and tail. Maybe because of the shape they make in flight, their wings held high above the horizontal.

The marsh hawk was here to remind me to learn to hover and to turn in flight. It was a Zen teaching. I am working on detachment. The marsh hawk brought me these lessons in a previous Shabbos walk but lately I'm failing miserably. This harrier was a sweet reminder that the Universe still wants me to get this right.

A family joined me on the viewing platform. They were looking for the eagle. They passed the same man on the trail.

"Have you seen it?" the father asked me.

"No," I said. "But I haven't really looked."

And I hadn't. I generally let *wochangi* direct me. Wochangi is a Lakota word that refers to a sacred power or influence. The Lakota know that each creature has a wochangi, according to its kind, and I know it, too. It's what guides my eyes to the hawks in the trees when I'm driving along the road and couldn't possibly see them otherwise. Wochangi is perceivable by soul. One can learn through wochangi if attentive and listening. The closer a creature is to an archetype, the greater the wochangi. The eagle, as the archetypal bird of prey, has tremendous wochangi. A red-tailed hawk has a lot, too; not as much as an eagle, but more than a red-shouldered. I can often feel the difference, even when I can't see it. Not always, though. I once mistook a crow for an immature bald eagle. But it *was* far away.

The eagle across the Great Marsh was way out of my wochangi range. It wasn't even visible to the naked eye. But the father was a regular. He knew where to look. He found it in his viewing glass. I took a look, too, through my binoculars. A mature bald eagle sat in the distance about a mile away. A tiny thing, but the stance, the distinct contrast of dark and white, was unmistakable. I lowered my glasses. The eagle definitely wasn't visible to a naked eye. But it was interesting to think that I was to it. In fact, it could probably see that I was writing. Surely it could see my fingers moving.

The father and I took different approaches. He wanted to see eagles. I wanted to discover them. And, more important to me than seeing eagles, was experiencing wildness.

I returned to my car, happy and satisfied. It had been a wonderful Shabbos walk. I drove to the visitor center in the state park. Chief Ranger Susan Lilly and her husband Johnny were walking me to an eagle nest. You couldn't find more gracious guides anywhere. Susan went way out of her way to accommodate my every need. Johnny pointed out my first red-headed woodpecker ever—we saw five or six as we walked along the park road—and helped me identify my first immature bald eagle in flight.

We started off through the woods. This part of the park was off-limits to visitors. As we approached the nest, I got excited. An average nest can weigh a ton. Eagles keep adding to them each year. As much as a foot. An eagle typically lives twenty to thirty years in the wild, but can live till fifty and has been known to survive as long as seventy-five years. They mate for life. The largest recorded nest was in Alaska. It weighed two and one half tons. It was nine and one-half feet wide and twenty feet deep. One of us could live in one of those.

Nests, called aeries, are built in very high trees near water. They are constructed from sticks, plants, and soft moss, with pine needles in the center. Eagles also like beds of pine.

We approached the vicinity of the nest. It seemed to me far from the water, but what's far when you can see a mile away and only have to fly to get there. Eagle nests are made in many different shapes: cylinders, bowls, upside-down cones. This one was shaped like a disk.

As we stood under the eagles' nest, the clouds thinned and moved. In those long few seconds, the sky turned blue.

If you go looking for an eagle and don't find one, pray for the nest. If you go looking for the nest and can't find it, pray for the tree. If you don't know where the tree is, pray for the forest.

bald eagle

Part Three: Canoe Ride

The next day, my host, Diana Rock, after cooking up an incredible Sunday brunch for her husband Walt, daughter Chelsea, and me, put two kayaks in her van and drove me to the park. Susan Lilly met us at the boat launch with Johnny and her son Elijah. Susan was a little leery of my taking myself out in a kayak for the first time ever and in frozen water with a relatively newly ruptured spinal disk. I guess I was a little leery, too, but was ready and willing just the same. I was dressed for the arctic, with five layers of clothing, two hats, and Diana's waterproof shoes. My dress made me feel ready for anything.

Diana, an experienced canoe guide and volunteer at the park, got in her kayak and waited for us in the bay. Elijah and I were put in the middle of the canoe sitting on the bottom, and Johnny and Susan paddled us off.

We had the bay to ourselves as we headed for Kane's Creek. The sound of the ice floes rolling over the tides was an incredible way to experience wildness.

A pair of belted kingfishers were the first to greet us. Their loud and noisy rattles, crested blue-gray heads and bodies, and white collars were diagnostic. Their big heads, short tails and feet, and long, sharp, thick beaks always look slightly, oddly, out of proportion, though perfectly proportioned for catching fish, which they do with remarkable speed and agility. Their sudden hovers and deep, irregular wingbeats make them predictably unpredictable and fun to watch. We lingered as they darted into the creek and up again, diving headlong from air to water.

Farther along, two mature bald eagles found their perch in trees on the edge of the water. As we approached, one took flight and we watched it fly to the other bank and find a tree with more cover, farther in from the creek. It is not possible to see those great wings take to the air at close range, and that striking white tail fly off, and not feel awe; nor to witness the commanding white head and dark body, perched upright, chest full, head alert, face intense, eyes penetrating: a consciousness both precise and comprehensive.

We passed a tree with three great blue herons hunkered down on branches reaching over the water. As we paddled by, only their feathers moved in the wind.

We were breaking ice with our paddles as we went along, and so delighting in the fact that Diana took photos of Johnny holding up pieces of sheets of ice.

In the winter chill, the creek was ours and the eagles'. We saw an immature fly overhead, and I caught several more adults perched deeper in the trees. A red-shouldered hawk slipped from view before we could get a really good look.

The ice thickened as the canoe scraped through the water farther up the creek. Wanting to push on, we respected the elements enough to keep us wise. We headed back, hugging the shoreline as close as ice would permit. The three great blues were still there, now joined by a fourth on a neighboring tree. Ice showed the shapes of logs that had floated away from it and places it had buckled around debris.

We were still and quiet as we rounded the curve back into the bay, each in our own place in wildness. Something begged silence in the frozen waters and in being the only unwinged two-leggeds to have passed by that day.

Part Four: The Two-Leggeds

I had arrived in the area on Christmas Day. I drove into the town of Occoquan, learning it was interesting, quaint and historic. This day it was all closed up, like a ghost town in a great freeze. Not one storefront, not one restaurant, not one business stirred. The streets and sidewalks were empty. The cars parked along the side of the road weren't going anywhere. I went looking for a place to stay, driving slowly up and down deserted streets. My tires were spinning and my car skidded on the icy roads. I couldn't find one hotel sign, guesthouse, or B&B. Not only was there no room at the inn; there was no inn.

That night I wound up staying at one of the huge chain hotels along the interstate. Minimal staff made for minimal amenities. Though I was near one of the largest shopping malls in the country, not one restaurant was open; not one vehicle moved. My Christmas dinner was the complimentary apples at check-in, smeared with peanut butter from the tiny tubs I wrested from a staffer who was stocking up for the morning's continental breakfast. It was the only food I had had since breakfast.

In the first room I was given, the heating unit wasn't working. In the second, the door didn't bolt. The third room looked out on blinding crime lights nine stories high. I closed the heavy curtains and hoped for the best. That night, in my nonsmoking room, as I prepared for bed, thick cigarette smoke wafted in through the bathroom air vents. I repacked my belongings, searched out four other rooms, and finally unpacked once again. Still awake at 2:30 A.M., I was not a happy camper.

You can imagine my delight, therefore, when I returned from my bird walk with Johnny the next day, and Susan told me she had found a place for me to stay: the guesthouse adjacent to the home of one of the community's movers and shakers. I was to learn she was also a gourmet cook, the town archivist and historian, an expert kayaker, and one of the most generous, fun-loving, and energetic women I had ever met. Her husband was also generous, fun-loving, and energetic, though he was napping when Susan led me to the house after dark. Indeed, it was Walt who welcomed me into his home, showed me to my quarters, and got me settled in. Walt not only designed his extraordinary house, he also played professional football for the Washington Redskins and the San Francisco 49ers.

After our canoe ride, Diana went home to prepare an impromptu dinner for all of us. Susan and I joined her in the kitchen around 5:30 where we chopped and sliced a little, and some of us sipped wine.

Diana was amazing to watch as she whipped up a feast before our eyes. Walt and Johnny hit it off watching sports, and Chelsea and Elijah were nowhere to be seen.

Two hours later, the food was in covered dishes on the sideboard and a festive table awaited. The dining room was still glowing with holiday cheer. Two days late, maybe, but I was getting a Christmas dinner after all. Mary Jane arrived just as we were sitting down to eat. Only then did I find out how this all came about.

Susan knew I was not prepared to spend another night at the hotel. She was reluctant to let me leave Mason Neck without seeing the park from a canoe. She called Mary Jane, past president of the Friends of Mason Neck. Mary Jane called Diana who was at the mall, shopping at Nordstrom. Sight unseen, Diana said yes.

It takes community to sustain community.

An ecosystem is about communities. Communities of plant and animal, water and soil, bird and tree, life co-existing, all needing the others for survival. In the midst of the gridlock and the high-occupancy-vehicle (HOV) lanes of the Beltway and Interstate 95, in one of the top five most congested metropolitan areas in the country, Mason Neck stands out as such a community. The people of Mason Neck also stand out, sticking their own necks out for a stranger passing through, offering food and shelter, warmth and friendship, giving refuge to a two-legged at holiday time.

It used to be that people lived in walled cities to keep the wild out. Beasts were everywhere feared, and safety from the wild was within the city walls, islands of culture and civilization sprinkled in the great wilderness of the world. Now it is wilderness that is walled. In places we call refuges, national forests, and parks, we have set aside islands of wilderness in the middle of human habitation. All we can do now is hope to preserve what remains. Wilderness as it was—worldwide—is forever gone. It is not in Africa or Asia or out there somewhere in the great wide world. The world isn't as wide as all that, and people and their need and greed are gobbling it up for their own consumption. It is disappearing even more rapidly outside the borders of these United States, where collectively we humans are annihilating more than twenty-seven thousand species of plants and animals a year.

In these days, it takes a community of people to preserve a community of wildness.

Mason Neck is such a community.

As I left my newly found feathered and unfeathered friends of Mason Neck, I drove past Gunston Hall Plantation. Gunston Hall is the ancestral home of George Mason IV, from whom the Neck takes its name. He was an author of the Virginia Bill of Rights, on which the United States Constitution's Bill of Rights is based. I can't help but feel the community of Mason Neck is writing another Bill of Rights, one for those who cannot speak for themselves. They are giving voice to the birds and animals, the trees and marshes, the bays and rivers, the living treasures of this planet, and the inheritance of all the peoples of the earth.

Diana pointed out, on the map and on our road tour, the three consecutive peninsulas jutting out into the Potomac: Mason Neck, Fort Belvoir, and Mount Vernon, where George Mason, Lord Fairfax, and George Washington once resided. She was fond of imagining them shouting to each other across the river, planning the great plans for this nation. In their day, they each practically owned their own peninsula, commanding lands and views of the water unheard of in our own time. How could they conceive of Beltways and HOV lanes, of human culture and civilization destroying the natural world they took for granted. But if they could have, and if they were here now, I would hope they would be crafting that Bill of Wildness Rights, and using all the power of the government and the people to enforce it. In their absence, we must do it, and we must do it now.

Acknowledgments: The author thanks Susan Lilly, Johnny Pilcicki, Diana Rock, Walt Rock, Stan Gray, and Mary Jane Reyes for their generosity and assistance in the preparation of this essay.

❧

Judith Kahn writes articles on the environment, spirituality, travel, and other subjects. Her work has appeared in the *New York Times, Esquire,* the *Miami Herald,* and numerous quarterlies. She is the author of the book *The Guide to Conscious Communication,* a published poet, and was a dance critic for *Dance* magazine. A book featuring eco-spirituality is currently under review for publication, and she is seeking a publisher for her animal stories, nature adventures, and tales of wandering. A former faculty member at the University of Virginia, she works as a consultant in leadership development, team building, curriculum planning, cultural communications, and environmental ethics. She holds a Ph.D. in psychology and religious studies and is an ordained rabbi.

The Nature Conservancy assisted in the establishment and growth of Mason Neck State Park and Mason Neck National Wildlife Refuge by acquiring a total of 2,970 acres beginning in 1967 and transferring the land to state and federal ownership.

INTO THE GREAT DISMAL
Great Dismal Swamp

Stefan Bechtel

If there were Druids whose temples were the oak groves, my
temple is the swamp.
    —Henry David Thoreau, *Journal*, January 4, 1853

Quarter moon rising amongst early autumn stars. Twilight. Silence. A light southwesterly breeze.

Thirty feet off our port bow, I can just discern the outline of my
fifteen-year-old son Adam, intrepid young voyager in his solo sea kayak,
making his way down along the south shore of the lake. He lifts his
paddle in rhythmic strokes across three stacked bands of light and
dark: the hazy shimmer of the water; the dark slash of the distant
tree line across the far shore; and the glimmering twilit sky.

It's a cool late September evening and we're adrift on Lake
Drummond, the vast, dark, extremely shallow and weirdly beautiful
lake at the center of the Great Dismal Swamp.

From time to time we drift past a great bald cypress marching out
into the lake, its twisted, phantasmal mass of roots and knees resembling the flying buttresses of a medieval cathedral. Before the swamp
was lumbered out, some of these trees grew so large that trappers

used the hollowed-out trunks as cabins. In the gloaming they look unearthly as baobabs on the African bushvelt.

Besides the dip and lift of our paddles, we can hear only a pair of screech owls calling back and forth out of the canebrake in their melancholy, descending tremolo, like the witch in *The Wizard of Oz* after she's been doused with a bucket of water: "I'm *melllting! I'm melllting!*"

It's the sense of vague dread in the screech owl's call, the deathly thrill that's always attracted a certain kind of person to the swamp (and repelled others from it). The young Robert Frost, spurned by a lover, came down here from Massachusetts in 1894 intending to commit sentimental suicide in the swamp. (He was instead sidetracked by a group of drunken duck hunters who whisked him off to Nags Head and the rest of his life.) And a celebrated 1803 poem by the Irish writer Thomas Moore, "The Lake of the Dismal Swamp," absolutely drips with romantic foreboding. It tells the story of an Indian maiden who died just before her wedding and is still sometimes seen paddling a ghostly white canoe across this very lake:

> But oft, from the Indian hunter's camp
>
> This lover and maid so true
> Are seen at the hour of midnight damp
> To cross the Lake by a fire-fly lamp
> And paddle their white canoe!

Plenty of people who've tramped and camped in the Dismal report having seen ghostly lights in the swamp. Like all swamps, it's given to glimmering with odd lights caused by foxfire, the luminescence given off by fungi in decaying wood, burning methane escaping from decomposing vegetation, or smoking, smoldering peat. The swamp, it seems, is a kind of translucent veil between the worlds.

The Most Remarkable Thing

On a map, the Dismal shows up as a great, dark, roughly rectangular roadless hole, straddling the Virginia–North Carolina line, just to the south and west of the Tidewater megalopolis of Hampton Roads–Norfolk–Virginia Beach. Depending on how you define it, estimates of the Dismal's total size range upwards of two hundred thousand acres—more than three hundred square miles. Lying so close to the periphery of civilization, it's located almost precisely where you'd expect to see a big international airport, surrounded by a sprawl of megamalls, surrounded by subdivisions. Instead, you find only darkness and silence: the two ripest, rarest prizes of modern life.

This has got to be one of the most remarkable things about this altogether remarkable place. Here we are on a three-thousand-acre lake on a pleasant Saturday night, less than twenty miles from a vast cityscape of more than 1.5 million inhabitants, and there's not a single light along the shore. No bass boats, no Jet Skis. No discount superstores. No human voice.

To be perfectly fair, this blessed silence has descended only after two boisterous canoe-loads of Boy Scouts returned to the public campground a half mile from the edge of the lake. And, of course, the swamp's delicious darkness has a good deal to do with the fact that 107,000 acres of it are now protected as a national wildlife refuge. A quarter century ago, almost 50,000 acres owned by Union Camp, the forest products company, were turned over to The Nature Conservancy and made into a refuge to be administered by the U.S. Interior Department's Fish and Wildlife Service. At the time, it was the largest single corporate land donation ever made to the American people for wildlife preservation.

This great gift was officially announced on George Washington's birthday, 1973, because most of the Union Camp land was once owned by George Washington himself. As a young man, he surveyed the swamp, camped on the shores of Lake Drummond and pronounced it "a glorious paradise." Then he promptly set about trying to make money off it. With other investors he set up two syndicates known as the Dismal Swamp Land Company and the Adventurers for Draining the Great Dismal Swamp. He attempted, without much success, to grow rice. Later, after discovering that juniper, cypress and other hardwoods would turn out to be the swamp's only real cash crops, he and his partners dredged the first of the great canals into the swamp, known to this day as Washington Ditch—probably the first physical monument in America bearing the name of the Father of Our Country.

"A Morass of Appalling Gloom"

Any wild place in America, particularly one a stone's throw from a major metropolis, can always benefit from some formidable barrier to entry to help ensure its survival. Snakes help (or even merely rumors of snakes). So do bugs, heat, brier thickets and a bad reputation. This wild place has been blessed with all that and, best of all, its wonderfully forbidding name: the Great Dismal Swamp. After all, who wants to go spend the weekend in a place world-famous for being dismal?

Its reputation as a bad place to spend the weekend has a long and celebrated history. Many nineteenth-century writers, already temperamentally inclined to melancholy hyperbole, pulled out all the stops when they started writing about the swamp. One who visited in 1888 described it as "a morass of forbidding and appalling gloom . . . the fecund bed of fever and malaria, infested with deadly serpents and wild beasts." Venomous water moccasins were said to drop out of overhanging trees into boats. The "miasmal vapors" of the swamp were said to be so overpowering that even birds wouldn't fly over it.

Colonel William Byrd, of Westover, is often credited with first using the word "dismal" to describe the swamp (though there are earlier uses of that appellation on record). In 1728 he published an account of the surveying party that first penetrated the swamp end to end, in order to establish the long-disputed border between North Carolina and Virginia. At that time, nobody knew how wide it was, so crossing the swamp was a daunting task. Byrd wrote of the men fighting their way through bamboo briers so thick "that there was no scuffing through them without the help of Pioneers"; of quagmires so moist and trembling "it was an easy Matter to run a ten-foot pole up to the Head in it"; of sleeping in places that "made a fitter lodging for Tadpoles than men." The party saw no animals at all, he wrote, because "doubtless the eternal Shade that broods over this mighty Bog, and hinders the sunbeams from blessing the Ground, makes it an uncomfortable Habitation for anything that has life."

By the ninth day, the party was exhausted, lost and nearly out of food. They began hungrily eyeing the camp dog. Then, to their "unspeakable comfort," they heard the lowing of cattle and the barking of dogs and knew they'd nearly reached the other side. They clambered onto firm ground, "which they embraced with as much Pleasure as Shipwrecked Wretches do the Shoar."

Byrd's colorful but inaccurate account of the swamp paints such a grim picture that some have speculated it might have been a negative marketing ploy to enable him and others to buy the land cheap. Because, as many other adventurers have discovered once they actually got here, the reality is quite different—neither as miasmal, nor as dreadful, as you may have heard.

"Scaring the Owl and Fox"

My son Adam, our dauntless guide Chuck Conley and I entered the swamp by stowing our gear into the watertight hatches in a pair of seventeen-foot plastic sea kayaks and slipping into the water of the Dismal Swamp Canal, which runs along the eastern edge of the swamp beside Route 17. Though it's possible to reach Lake Drummond on foot (there are about one hundred miles of hiking trails in the swamp), probably the easiest way to get to the heart of it is by boat, using the network of manmade canals and "feeder ditches" that crisscross the swamp. As swamps go, the Dismal is not terribly wet much of the year—in fact, the canals were built not only to transport lumber out of the swamp but also to maintain water levels so as to keep the vast beds of flammable peat wetted down and fire resistant. Slipping into the swamp by boat, you hardly have the sensation of being in a swamp at all, but rather of floating through dense woods.

Once the roar of Route 17 fades away, we're met with little sound but muted birdsong and the dip-splash of our own paddles. The swamp is a lot quieter than it was two hundred years ago, when a whole cottage industry grew up around the excellent, rot-resistant lumber of cypress and juniper (also known as Atlantic white cedar, or swamp cedar), which was used for shingles, crates, barrels and tubs. This canal we're paddling down was once a kind of inland interstate used by shallow-draft, flat-bottomed "lighters" carrying loads of juniper shingles out of the swamp. In fact, though it's now just a footnote in the history of American inland navigation, the Dismal Swamp Canal is the oldest continuously used manmade waterway in American history. It was built around 1800 to connect the Chesapeake Bay to the north with Albemarle Sound, in North Carolina, to the south, to help spread economic prosperity to both places. Among the canal's most enthusiastic supporters was Thomas Jefferson, who wrote that the canal project "is the only speculation in my life I have decidedly wished to be engaged in."

Later, rickety little narrow-gauge trains, also built to transport shingles out of the swamp, added to the din. In 1830 a passenger railroad crossed the northern edge of the swamp between Suffolk and Portsmouth. Mourning the coming of railroads to such wild places, Thoreau wrote in *Walden*, in 1854: "Far through unfrequented woods on the confines of towns, where once only the hunter penetrated by day, in the darkest night dart these bright saloons without the knowledge of their inhabitants; this moment stopping at some brilliant station-house in town or city, where a social crowd is gathered, the next in the Dismal Swamp, scaring the owl and fox."

Tumbling down over both banks of the now-silent, coffee-colored canal are dense lowland woods known as *pocosin*, an Indian word meaning "impenetrable thicket." In places they look riotous as a rain forest, thick with switch cane, sweet pepperbush, orange-throated jewelweed and sassafras and fragrant wax myrtle, which supplies the scent in bayberry candles. Partly because they're so impenetrable, the Dismal's pocosins shelter a profusion of life, including thirty species of ferns, and such rare southern exotica as the May-blooming wild or silky camellia and the dwarf trillium. The swamp is also home to about eighty-five species of nesting songbirds and one of the largest native breeding populations of black bear in the East, estimated in one recent census at about three hundred animals.

We pass a couple of big tumbledown tupelos, their roots wrenched from the ground by a recent nor'easter—poignant reminders of our proximity to the ocean, which is only about thirty miles to the east of here. The moderating influence of the warm Gulf Stream keeps the swamp more temperate than inland areas at this latitude, so that you find plants and animals here that you don't normally find in much profusion this far north—Spanish moss, for instance. In fact, the whole swamp is a complex ecological crossroads of northern and southern species. As a preserve, it's especially significant because it contains an array of different ecosystems, from evergreen shrub bogs to loblolly pine barrens, bald cypress swamps to brier thickets.

Six Weird Things about the Dismal

Besides the silence and the stillness, there are many other odd and interesting things about this place:

1. Most swamps are shallow catch basins with streams flowing into them. But when twenty-one-year-old George Washington surveyed

the Dismal in 1763, he was surprised to discover that rivers ran *out* of the swamp, not into it. He reported that the swamp was "neither a plain nor a hollow, but a hillside." Lake Drummond, instead of being its lowest point, is one of the highest—actually twenty or thirty feet above sea level.

2. Lake Drummond is one of only two natural lakes in the state of Virginia (the other being Mountain Lake, in Giles County). Its origins are still mysterious, though it's known to retain water because of a one-hundred-fifty-foot-thick bed of heavy clay that sits underneath its peaty bottom like a cup. One theory is that Lake Drummond was created when a saltwater bay gradually closed in on its seaward side or perhaps was dammed off by beavers. Another theory is that the lake was created by a meteor strike—and, in fact, local Indian legends say it was created by a "firebird."

3. The water is stained so dark with tannins from the swamp that when sunlight strikes its surface it looks like chocolate asphalt. Stick your hand six inches into the drink and it disappears. Pouring out of the spillway at the dam by the Dismal Swamp campground, the water looks like fifty gallons a second of Starbucks espresso.

In effect, the water really is a kind of swamp coffee because it turns that color from percolating through beds of peat and the roots and bark of gum, cypress, maple and juniper trees. It's a brew so dark and strong, in fact, that a species of blind fish lives here. The species is known as the Dismal Swamp fish (*Chologaster cornuta*), and it probably does not know that most of its relatives live in caves.

In the old days this curious stuff was called "juniper water" and was said to have remarkable healing powers, including the ability to cure malaria. Casks of it were loaded on ships to be taken on sea voyages because it would not go bad (the tannins make it acidic, thus acting as a kind of natural antibiotic). It has a flat aftertaste, a little like weak tea, but is otherwise quite refreshing.

4. One of the oddest things about the lake is what is *not* here. Because of the darkness and acidity of the water, very little aquatic

vegetation grows here, hence surprisingly few fish or waterfowl can be found here. It's easy to imagine this place absolutely aswarm with geese and ducks and the long-legged waders. But we only see one osprey, a kingfisher, a couple of cormorants and a great egret winging across the distant tree line, its white wingbeats regular as heartbeats. There are also common loons on the lake, which Chuck says he sees in the swamp almost year-round.

Old-timer birdman Brooke Meanley, a government biologist and lifelong lover of the great southern swamps, called this "the Great Songbird Swamp." That's partly because of all the songbirds that breed here, but also because so few waterfowl actually nest here. Mostly they just pass through or overwinter, like the blizzards of snow geese who put down on these waters when the weather turns cool. "The student of the geographic distribution of birds will be more impressed by the absence of species he would expect to find here than by the presence of those he does find," Meanley wrote.

5. There are no rocks in the Dismal, Chuck says. Those things that look like rocks are only chunks of peat rolling drowsily in the shallows of the canals, like elephant dung.

6. When the Dismal Swamp Canal was being re-dredged around the turn of the century, steam shovels began pulling up enormous oyster shells out of the muck. Some were a foot long and weighed five pounds apiece. They were thousands of years old, dating from the time the Nansemond escarpment that now forms the western edge of the swamp was a beach of the Atlantic Ocean. In many places the ground is still littered with (smaller) ancient oyster shells, though the open ocean now lies far to the east. There's no longer any salt or brackish water in the swamp: it's all fresh.

A Caterwauling in the Canebrake

It's an easy four-mile paddle from our put-in, near Arbuckle Landing, to the small campground beside the dam near Lake Drummond, which is the only (legal) place to camp in the swamp. We put ashore beside the spillway, where there's a boat trolley to transport small motorboats over the dam, a small dam keeper's house, fire pits and outhouses. The dam keeper, a morose-looking man wearing a tattered seed cap, shows up in a motorized jon boat on Sunday morning carrying a bag of groceries and the newspaper. He's enthusiastic about his day.

black bear

"It's a good job," he says. "Real quiet."

There's lots of deer and wild turkey out here, he says, as well as foxes (gray and red) and bobcat. River otters come to cavort in the churn below the dam, and there are still mink in the swamp. And though for some reason they've never discovered the trash cans at the campground, there are lots of bears. He says the bears will swim across the canals to get into nearby cornfields, destroying a city block of corn in a night. Last year one farmer (having secured a kill permit to put away a "nuisance" animal) shot an eight-hundred-pound bear.

"It's a shame anybody has to kill a beautiful animal like that just to kill it," he says. "But the thing that really got me was that they just let it lay there in the water."

Later on, Chuck confides, "Just so you know: the first time I heard that story, the bear weighed four hundred pounds."

Despite its reputation, we find the swamp to be quite hospitable to humans as well as bears. It helps that we've waited for the sweaty tidewater heat to break before making the trip, of course. It also helps that we've timed our trip for maximum bug avoidance (during July and August the yellow flies are said to be voracious, but during this trip, though I came prepared to fight the Battle of the Bugs, I never once uncorked my DEET). The water in Lake Drummond is delightfully cool, being partially spring fed, despite the late-summer heat and the fact that the lake is hardly anywhere deeper than six feet. The lake bottom is pleasantly sandy. And, of course, we find no "eternal Shade" in the swamp (though Route 17 is so densely overgrown that signs remind travelers to keep their headlights on even by day).

It's true that there are at least three kinds of poisonous snakes in the swamp: canebrake rattlers (a southern variant of the timber rattler), cottonmouths and copperheads. But Chuck says in dozens of trips out here he's never seen a rattler and only occasionally seen a copperhead or cottonmouth. The only kind we see during our two days in the Dismal is a harmless northern water snake, its small beadlike head breaking the surface of the shallows, zigzagging along, unzipping the lake.

In the spring of the year, all sins are forgiven; life is lush, the living is easy. Now it's early fall, and the swamp has begun to bestow its blessings again. The beastly heat is beginning to break. The bugs are mostly gone. And the fruit is ripe on the vine.

Curtains of blue-black scuppernong grapes dangle over the dark water. You grab them by the handful, spit out the seeds and skins and savor the last sweetness of summer. Here and there along the sandy shore we find fallen pawpaws, some half-nibbled, some firm and full as runty little yellowish cucumbers. When you break them open they're filled with a kind of foamy yellow banana custard. They have small flat seeds, similar to persimmon seeds.

In the gray, sandy leaf litter of the canal bank we find bear tracks and a couple of freshly broken pawpaw branches where the bears, too, have had an autumn feast. Chuck has seen nine bears in all his trips out here, mostly swimming across the canals. We don't see any, but one afternoon, walking along the woods by Washington Canal, we hear a hair-raising caterwauling back in the canebrake. It sounds like an angry bear, or maybe two angry bears, or a sow getting its throat cut. Maybe even the Swamp Thing. Anyhow, nothing good.

So we slip back to the beached boat, paddle back to camp, pack up our gear. It's time to get going anyhow.

On the way back up the feeder ditch toward the Dismal Swamp Canal and home, we spot a pond slider lurking up under the brush along the canal bank. It's a huge, handsome thing, its shell big as a dinner plate, with fierce yellow markings around its eyes and a plastron yellow as butter. These are the famous "dime-store" turtles, which used to be sold by the thousands at Woolworth's until the practice was outlawed.

Adam is entranced, so I unleash my inner child, climb out of the boat and grab the turtle for a closer look. It's oddly docile. Turning it over in my hands, I notice a deep, ragged gash across its carapace: collision with a powerboat prop. Exuding out of the gash is a sac of pink tissue, like a collapsed bubble-gum bubble. Suddenly it inflates, and I realize with a start that it's the turtle's exposed lung.

Such a beautiful, mysterious, damaged thing! Like all wild things, including this swamp, the turtle is as lovely as it is vulnerable, its life separated from its death by a film thin as paper. I bend down and release the turtle back into the water. As it sinks out of sight into the dismal darkness, I see the pink, extruded lung inflate once more, like a life raft.

And then it disappears.

Stefan Bechtel is a lifelong swamp lover who lives with his family in Charlottesville. He is the author or co-author of five books, including *Katherine: It's Time, The Good Luck Book,* and *The Practical Encyclopedia of Sex and Health,* which has sold more than 850,000 copies and been translated into Korean, Chinese, and Polish. He is a founding editor of *Men's Health* magazine. His work has appeared in *Esquire, Reader's Digest, American Way*, the *Washington Post*, and other publications.

Great Dismal Swamp National Wildlife Refuge was established in 1974 when The Nature Conservancy conveyed to the U.S. Department of the Interior a donation of nearly fifty thousand acres that the Conservancy had received from the Union Camp Corporation. The Conservancy continues to acquire nearby lands for the purpose of expanding the refuge.

LOSS AND RECOMPENSE AT THE PINNACLE

The Pinnacle, Clinch River

Garvey Winegar

Who said nature heals?
Heals what? one might reasonably ask.
Itself? Us?

That's expecting a lot from a 208-acre section of trees, rocks, some cliffs, a stream and a smattering of rare and endangered plants and freshwater mussels that have their own problems.

Bear with me. If you detect an undercurrent of despair, then you've picked up on part of what I was feeling as I parked my four-wheel-drive at the end of the road beside the waterfall on Big Cedar Creek.

After all, I was entering the Pinnacle State Natural Area Preserve in a section of Russell County in southwest Virginia. The Pinnacle and the rest of southwest Virginia have taken some hard knocks in the past 150 years.

Also on this day, I was in the process of losing a friend and constant companion of a dozen years. Within the hour, Jack would be dead.

Never hurts to enter one of Virginia's scenic and rare natural areas with what Lyndon Johnson called "a heavy heart."

* * *

First, about Jack . . .

Though he possessed a pedigree considerably longer and more impressive than his master's, his everyday name was Jack the Brittany. Expressive amber eyes. Soft coat of brown and white. A gentle soul (except around other dogs) whose one aim in life was to please. He'd make sure he had your permission before he did almost anything, even eating, which is more than I can say for my three children.

In twelve years, he and I covered some ground. Jack pointed grouse in the Blue Ridge and quail in Tidewater Virginia, but he also found fishing intensely interesting and would lean far out over the bank of a pond or river, trembling with excitement, on the infrequent occasions when I reeled in a bass or trout.

fish and mussels

To be sure, Jack was eccentric, but that too fit my style. He'd thump the side of the bed at dawn each morning, thus eliminating the need for an alarm clock. He'd point grasshoppers as readily as anything else, and as much as he wanted constant attention, he'd lean away as you stroked him. If a car door were left open, you'd find him sitting in the back like a potentate, waiting for whatever adventure lay ahead. He absolutely, positively hated being alone.

After two strokes and an advancing unidentified illness, Jack needed help getting down the back steps each morning. Level ground was all right, but his legs and brain got tangled with opposing signals when it came to porch steps.

I'd walk him around in the yard and let him pee. If we were lucky, he'd come across the faint aroma of black bear on the back lawn. Bear often wander through during the night from adjoining Shenandoah National Park.

The old hunting genes would fire like synapses. His shoulder hair would bristle, and a deep rumble would come from somewhere inside that doomed chest. "Good dog," I'd say. "You look like you're ready to tackle a bear." The beautiful amber eyes, for a moment, were alert again. He'd spin and throw dust and growl a little more and pee again, and we'd go back in the house where he'd sleep beside my desk for the remainder of the day.

But Jack was dying. Cancer, most likely. He was too old and too feeble to endure the ordeal of surgery, so we'd kept him comfortable and petted and loved him a lot during the last few months. We knew he'd tell us when it was time to go, and he did.

"Today," he'd said in his own way to my wife Deane back in Waynesboro. It's time to go. Today.

This, of course, was the day I'd chosen to go to The Pinnacle, and not entirely by accident. I'd been on a trip to southwest Virginia for several days, but Deane and I had stayed in frequent contact by phone because of Jack. She was taking him to the vet for medication every morning. The vet agreed that day with Jack's decision that the time had come.

A confession is in order. I wanted to be somewhere else when the day and hour arrived to carry Jack into the vet's office for the last time. I knew I'd be a basket case. Though compassion and love dictated that it must be done, putting down (a fine euphemism for killing) my own dog would just about reduce me to blubbering jelly. I didn't think I could do it, or even be a part of it. Deane loved Jack no less than I, but she is the stronger of the two of us when it comes to this sort of thing.

Best, I thought, to take the coward's way out and seek refuge in a remote section of mountain alongside a clear trout stream, where there were no slack bundles to carry home and no graves to be dug, and no witnesses to what might be unmanly breakdowns.

So while parked on a side street in nearby Lebanon, before leaving the last cell with enough strength to transmit a phone call, she and I made the agonizing decision over a distance of almost four hundred miles. She'd do it. Alone. I, in turn, would take the rocky, rutted road into Pinnacle Natural Area, alternately relieved and depressed, expecting nothing.

* * *

The Pinnacle, as it's known to local people in Russell County, isn't exactly on the superhighway of life. For those traveling I-81 a few miles to the east, the area would define "off the beaten path" quite nicely.

The dirt road in requires slow, low-gear driving. You could bring in a Buick if you knew what you were doing. But a Blazer would serve better.

Big Cedar Creek sometimes runs beside the road and sometimes in it. The creek, though gin-clear, pristine and shallow in summer, will occasionally go on a rampage. Over the years, it has washed the road away to bedrock in places. Stretches of the road are like driving on cobblestones, except that these cobblestones are rounded river rocks the size of cantaloupes.

One spring two years ago, I tried to reach Pinnacle Natural Area but high water from a recent storm was roaring down Big Cedar Creek. The entrance was blocked. Even Moses would have hesitated.

It's just as well. At that time, I was little more than curious about this unique preserve that I'd heard several people mention—people whose opinion about wild places I respect.

On this trip, however, I needed to think, reflect, even grieve. This time I needed solitude, and from every indication, I would have it. Not a single wet tire track led out of the river crossing. It appeared that, on this weekday, I'd be the only person in the entire natural area.

That was fine. I didn't feel like talking, even if I came across someone kind enough to listen to my babbling.

* * *

Pinnacle Natural Area is in the mountains, and mountains place a
distinctive imprint on life that chooses or is forced to live there.

Deltas, plains and open spaces give the appearance, real or imag-
ined, of being all-encompassing, unlimited, expansive.

By comparison, mountains divide, isolate, separate. I wandered
along several of the walking trails through hollows, across ridges and
beneath six-hundred-feet-high dolomite cliffs, thinking that in every
direction, there's a mountain rampart that was extremely hard to get
around, over or through until recent times. If you were one of the
early settlers drifting south and west in the mid-1700s and peeled off
the Wilderness Road, which later became US 11, you might expect,
even welcome, a certain isolation from your neighbors a few hollows
or mountaintops away.

In the natural world, a similar thing happens. Something found
here at the Pinnacle—plants such as tufted hairgrass or animals such
as the spiny riversnail—may not exist at all a few ridges or coves over.

In fact, the very uniqueness of this remote region sets it apart
from other areas and almost demands that it be protected from further degradation, such as the extensive logging that denuded much of
the East in the early twentieth century.

The area's calcium-rich bedrock, rich cove woodlands, limestone
cliffs, ridgetop glades and cascading streams such as Big Cedar encourage the survival of several unusual ferns and wildflowers, as well
as rare animal species.

The clear, clean waters of Big Cedar Creek support stocked trout,
and anglers travel here to catch them. But the creek probably had a
good natural supply of native brook trout at one time.

Native trout, however, like lots of other things in nature, were too fragile, too trusting, for man's heavy acquaintance. Natural food in any mountain stream is not abundant, so a native brookie would hit almost anything. One person with a can of worms and a cane pole could fish out a stream, provided he had the time and inclination. That's just what happened in many mountain streams.

Extensive logging and farming also took a toll as silt, fertilizers and cow poop mingled in pristine creeks and rivers. It has been a long time, however, since anyone raised tobacco or corn in the area of the Pinnacle. And since timbering is long past, and there are no upstream industries to dump garbage in the rivers, Big Cedar Creek and the Clinch River into which the creek flows are pure enough today to sustain one of the richest freshwater mussel populations to be found in the world.

For example, the delicate birdwing pearlymussel lives in only one other river in the world. Other rare river critters requiring the exquisite set of conditions found here include several other mussels, the spiny softshell turtle and the hellbender. The Pinnacle area is home to twelve rare plant species, five rare mollusks, two rare animals and two distinct natural communities.

* * *

I wish I could say that I found, then walked away from, a birdwing pearlymussel after I took the path down the hill to the confluence of bubbling Big Cedar and the placid Clinch River. But I did not, though I sat on river rocks and looked into the water for a long, long time. Once, a few years ago, I did some snorkeling with biologists very near here in the Clinch and discovered an underwater world that I didn't know existed, even through I grew up on the North Fork of the Holston River just a few miles west.

I fear that my people's attitude—isolated, Scots-Irish, God-fearing Baptists—was exactly the same as that described by Aldo Leopold in *A Sand County Almanac* when he wrote fifty years ago: "Conservation is getting nowhere because it is incompatible with our Abrahamic concept of land. We abuse land because we regard it as a commodity belonging to us. When we see land as a community to which we belong, we may begin to use it with love and respect."

Aldo, we have made some progress. If we hadn't, places such as the Pinnacle that were almost lost would be ski slopes or campgrounds. Now they're set aside as state preserves so that the fragile mussels and plants—this unusual ecosystem—have a modicum of protection.

People use the area, sure. Trash barrels overflow with picnic leftovers near the waterfall, and you'll see an empty beer can or a cigarette butt now and then along the Clinch River Trail. The place is used, but reasonably safe.

I wandered along the flowing river, the cliffs, the walking trails with their mountain backdrops on a very bad day to assuage a loss that's still difficult to talk about. Did it help coming here?

Maybe.

Is this a place to which I'd like to return at a happier time?

Certainly. No question.

And I'm equally certain of this: Jack, a born devotee of things natural and wild, would have loved it here.

Garvey Winegar, a native of southwest Virginia's Scott County, has been the senior outdoors columnist for the *Richmond Times-Dispatch* for more than a decade. He has been widely published in outdoor magazines and has won numerous state and national awards in his thirty years as an outdoor writer. He and his wife Deane are co-authors of *Highroad Guide to the Virginia Mountains* and *Natural Wonders of Virginia: Parks, Preserves, and Wild Places*.

The Pinnacle State Natural Area Preserve was established in 1989 and has since been expanded to 448 acres through the cooperative efforts of The Nature Conservancy, Russell County, and the Virginia Department of Conservation and Recreation.

HOME GROUND

FOREST CHILDREN
Fan Mountain

Susan Tyler Hitchcock

Almost twenty years ago, when my husband and I, newly wed, started looking for a piece of land to call home, we had a short list of all that we wanted: some forest, some pasture, some water, and some privacy. I don't even remember that we had children on our minds.

We spent a year looking. Real estate agents took us from one end of Albemarle County to the other. We hiked up mountains. We walked down dirt roads. We looked at houses and we looked at house sites, at two-acre lots and at hundred-acre farms. After all that looking around, we finally came back to the little piece of forest that some friends were willing to sell us.

They owned about forty acres in southern Albemarle County, up on Fan Mountain, a scalloped ridge south of Charlottesville. Look on the map created by the U.S. Geological Survey, and you find the area called "Fan Mountains," each wiggle of the scallop accorded its own identity. The tallest of them, says that 1967 map, is Mount Oliver, although you'll never hear any local use that name. Atop its peak sits the University of Virginia's observatory, built in the 1960s to support research in parallax astronomy. Three telescopes capture time-lapse night-sky images, comparing them to compute the distance from earth to stars. The biggest of those telescopes dominates the top of the mountain, a great white dome visible for miles around.

In the days when we first bought our forest land, the nearby town of Covesville had a country store, owned and operated by Duval Johnson, who had done so for forty years. The front door creaked and the wood floors sloped and it smelled of old food inside, but it was in Mr. Johnson's store that you felt the heartthrob of Covesville. When we first moved there, Duval Johnson still salted, sugared, and smoked old hams in the little block building out back. He still offered credit to Covesville residents who would walk from home to the store, along the same footpaths that they used before four-laning US 29 cut the town in two. The credit Mr. Johnson offered kept some of those folks going from one monthly check to the next.

In those days, the post office still operated out of a corner of Johnson's Store. Customers and postmaster glimpsed each other through a brass grille. Stamps, coins, money orders, and envelopes passed back and forth under that grille, wearing a smooth, organic curve down into the wooden counter like the curve worn into the stone steps of an ancient cathedral.

At Johnson's Store, you could get people talking about Fan Mountain. Half a dozen households dotted the lower stretches of the three-mile road that twisted up the mountain to the observatory. One half-crazy woman was building an A-frame up the ridge all by herself. Other than those homes, and the caretaker's house, right next to the observatory, Fan Mountain was a solid stretch of forest, hundreds of acres, new growth, but vigorous, strong, and wild.

In the first half of the century, people told me, Fan Mountain looked entirely different. Apple orchards extended from the foot almost up to the peak of the mountain. Trucks hauled bushel boxes, laden down with Winesaps and Albemarle pippins, to the cider mill or the packing shed or the brandy distillery, eight miles away in North Garden. Trains pulled in and out of Covesville, loaded down with apples. Some years back, Mr. Johnson told me, he had owned the property we were buying. Ran the orchard there with some business associates. Called that orchard "Dixie."

"Used to be that whole mountainside was covered with apple trees," Postmaster Drumheller told me. He swept his thick fingers across the view out the window, across all the expanse of Fan Mountain we could see. He rummaged through a drawer and pulled out a faded picture postcard. Red-dirt road, grass between the wheel tracks, apple trees puffed up with pink blossoms as far as the camera could see. "Covesville, Virginia," the postcard was labeled. Back then, this was an address to make a person proud.

* * *

There was little left of Dixie in the property we purchased. One craggy apple tree still clung to the bank of a stream, a spot where no one would have chosen to plant it. That lone remaining volunteer produced a few barely edible apples our first year there, then succumbed to trunk rot and tumbled down, last vestige of orchard days gone by.

Our sixteen acres offered what we wanted: forest, pasture, water, privacy. Our driveway followed an old county roadbed, abandoned when they paved a straighter highway. It meandered through a canopy of branches—oak, tulip poplar, hickory, with a few grand black cherries towering above and a pleasing cushion of redbud and dogwood down under. To get to our new land, we forded a stream and followed the overgrown track of an old orchard roadbed, up to a point where it crested and disappeared. There, on the right, rose a thirty-foot double chokecherry, two muscular trunks entwining like honeysuckle up a fence post. One other tall tree, a great red oak, stood solitary amidst a scrubby seedling hillside, densely scattered with blackberry, sumac, sassafras, locust, tree of heaven.

It was messy and scruffy and even a little sad, that clearing with two trees and the rest just underbrush struggling to gain a hold. Rocks pressed up out of red-ocher soil, soil that seemed thin and barren, as if orchard labors had spent all its topsoil. Just above the red oak, though, the forest shadows deepened. Of the hourglass shape that was our property, half contained that scraggly hillside and the other half stretched up to encompass rich, dark woods. We could follow the ghost of another orchard road up alongside a rock-strewn stream and soon stand amidst great trees—sweet birch, tulip poplar, shagbark hickory, paulownia, even an occasional American elm.

Of course it wasn't virgin forest. We saw signs of earlier use. Here would be a rock pile: belly-big boulders stacked three or four deep, an ancient human effort at clearing to work the soil. There would be a lopped-off treetop: limbs that once reached skyward now sprawled, sheared flat on the nether end and toppled headfirst into a crevice, rotting and crumbling, joining the soil. This mountain had been cleared, planted, and timbered. Many had come before, and yet now it felt so still. Nature endured.

From the roadbed, I liked to angle up steeper terrain, where neither apple wagon nor logging truck had ever ventured. There are slopes on Fan Mountain that rise a good sixty degrees, where you have to plant your boots sideways and grab on to saplings. This is where I drew in closest to the mountain, where shy bloodroot and black cohosh and rattlesnake plantain sank tender roots into the soil. I would scoop up a handful of that black soil and smell it: Porters loam, loose and crumbly, soul of the earth, full of the spice of sassafras and the rich rot of American chestnuts fallen a century ago. On such sheer slopes I even found the occasional ginseng: elusive, magical American mandrake, too precious to pull.

* * *

We sculpted our home site right on the tree line, looking down across the clearing, looking up into forest shade. Our first winter there, we had built the skeleton of a structure, but we slept and ate and washed in our "Silver Bullet," a thirty-foot Airstream trailer backed in between the trees. By our second summer there, the house was closed in and our son, John, was born. Two springs later, the house had an upper story and we had a daughter, Alison.

From the beginning, I invited my children into the forest. I remember one glorious, brisk summer day, just weeks after John was born. Wanting to shake the housebound feeling of new motherhood, I tucked my baby into our blue corduroy snuggle-pack and walked high up the mountain behind our home, straight up, past great stone monuments, shards and slices leaning in on one another, jutting out of the mountain floor. I reached a point where—wonder of wonders—after having seen nothing but forest looking up and looking down, I could peer down over the treetops and spy the tiny rooftop of our own house. I have never found that vantage point again, in all my walks up and down the mountain.

wild turkey

The work of building was not over when the children arrived. We had a deck on our house, but no railing. We had a back door that stepped out into space. We had stacks of lumber all around us. Sometimes, when David and I would move a pile of lumber, a dirt-red copperhead would slink away, robbed of its cool, shady shelter. Just as often, when I would heave a boulder onto the rubble wall forming up along the driveway, a glossy black widow spider would cling to its underside. It's a wonder our children didn't toddle into trouble, growing up as they did at the confluence of an unfinished house and raw nature. But they managed. They maneuvered. They learned to balance. They played in the woods.

As our children began to walk and to talk, the mountain landscape became their own. Early in the morning, I would point out the front window and lead their gaze down the hill toward two young deer, graceful and attentive. We would walk up the mountain, seeking shade in the midst of a hot summer's day. Our own noise would evoke a great flapping. We would stand, and listen, and then the dark form of a turkey would sweep up and away, abandoning ground litter for a treetop's safe haven. Bird sounds filled the air around us. Tom turkeys gobbled in the spring. Pileated woodpeckers drummed on tree trunks. Screech owls whinnied mournfully. My children learned to listen, and to name the disembodied sounds.

Forest animals shared our landscape—or rather, we shared theirs. Raccoons, opossums, skunks, squirrels, mice, voles. Crows, hawks, mourning doves, turkey vultures, an occasional great horned owl. Skinks and snakes. Box turtles, snapping turtles. Animals of pleasure and animals of pain. Grasshoppers, katydids, praying mantids, walking sticks, ladybugs, paper wasps, click beetles, fireflies. The world buzzed brightly, obliviously around us.

Often on a walk down our roadway at just the right time of year, we would startle an entire turkey brood: eight or ten little ones, fuzzy heads swiveling, skittling and hopping along, madly following mother out of our sight. Some animals would stop and turn and let us look closely. Bats and phoebes, mice and opossums have come into our home. John once twined a black snake around his neck. Another time, the children came upon a fawn. She sat, trembling and vulnerable, by the side of the driveway. They dared to touch her. They lifted and stroked her, feeling the fragile bonework, the beating heart, beneath her dewy fur. Still innocent, she accepted their attention. They touched her reality, then they placed her back into the forest, knowing that somewhere close by a mother deer was standing and watching, invisible, concerned.

* * *

Children grow up so quickly. Their world expands beyond the horizon they see. In this world of ours, too soon they come to crave speed and distance. They want to travel. First trikes and bicycles, skates and skateboards, on the path to automobiles. As my children discovered each new way to leave home, I heard a cacophony of complaining. "We should pave our driveway." "We need sidewalks." "We should live closer to other kids." "We should move into town."

I listened and smiled and, for the time being, kept my thoughts to myself. True enough, for the sake of a go-cart or roller skates or even a bike, it would be better to live in a house right next door to other houses, with a sidewalk reaching from the front door out to a sidewalk stretching up and down this block, and the next, and the next. Miles of sidewalk, blocks of houses. It's a childhood landscape I remember. In many ways, it would make life easier. The children could take off out the door to play with friends in the neighborhood. I wouldn't have to drive so long and so often.

Yet I know there's a reason we raised our children in the country.

Looking back through time, the years of parenting look so short now. We are already past the halfway mark. Looking forward, I am filled with wonder, pride, and a glint of pain as I glimpse the time, not far from now, when our adult children will leave this home, skid down the driveway, and make their own ways—into some other forest, or some other town, or some big city many miles away, where they ride subways to work and walk dogs on a leash and take elevators up to tiny apartments, locking and bolting the door behind them, closing the window to reduce the din of trucks and sirens, brakes and horns from street traffic below. It may be their choice.

And then, of what we have given them, what will remain? A memory of the forest. The quiver of wild animal heartbeat through warm fur. The smell of new snow. The sound of a rushing stream after rainfall. The shy surprise of springtime bloodroot in bloom. Dawn and the song of the wood thrush.

We have raised our children into a world of nature. They have grown up knowing that a forest is there, a forest far bigger than our backyard. We have tried to make theirs a caring and deliberate knowing. Name the trees and the insects and the flowers. Respect their ways of living, growing, dying. Understand how humans fit into the larger world.

I trust that when my children look back with adult perspective, they will thank us for the few short years during which their world was a forest, with a rock pile, a dirt road, a steep mountain slope, a thick patch of blackberries they could call their own. Childhood landscapes may drop out of conscious view, but they emanate influence throughout one's lifetime. Having known the forest as home, may our children always value the wild. If they live to see it threatened, may passion well up from deep within, from that place before words, and may they act upon that passion to see that nature not only survives but prevails in the world of their future, as it did in the world of their past.

Susan Tyler Hitchcock has written six books, including *Coming About: A Family Passage at Sea, Gather Ye Wild Things: A Forager's Year,* and her most recent book, *The University of Virginia: A Pictorial History.* She lives with her family on Fan Mountain in Covesville, south of Charlottesville. She also writes a column for *Albemarle* magazine called "Letters from Home."

ESCAPE TO NORTH RIVER GORGE
North River Gorge

Deane Winegar

Three hummingbird-size stones. Jawbone. Dog biscuits. Pocket tape recorder. Magnifier. Geology map, field guide and *Mountains of the Heart* by Scott Weidensaul. Two sandwiches, apple, slice of chocolate cake, water bottle.

Now there's an eclectic array of objects. Most of them come from dumping out the pockets of my jeans and belt pack. The last ones are the contents of my lunch bag. They're laid out beside me on a tablelike slab of rock in the middle of North River. Or what's left of North River in the midst of a stubborn summer drought.

The spot I've chosen for lunch is familiar. Gina Shepherd and I were here a few weeks ago, she with her two Brittanies, I with my black terrier, Toby. Besides being a good friend and hiking buddy, Gina is a teacher and outdoor writer extraordinaire, and she likes her sandwiches cut in triangles. There was water enough in the river then for two women and their dogs to paddle about without scraping bedrock. Today, the dwindling pool beneath the rock is sufficient only to cool my dangling feet.

The three stones and tape recorder on the corners of the unfolded map anchor it against the occasional little puff of wind in North River Gorge. I munch on the apple as I trace with one finger the yellow line representing the gorge.

The North River begins life as a spring atop Shenandoah Mountain in Augusta County, a mile south of Reddish Knob and scarcely more than a stone's throw from the West Virginia line. After descending from four thousand feet, the river's downward progress is interrupted by dams that form two cold lakes, drawing trout anglers to this part of the Dry River Ranger District of the George Washington National Forest. When the river regains its identity below the second dam, it turns northward, seeking lower ground.

Over the millennia, the tumbling water has carved a four-mile pass into bedrock to form North River Gorge, where I'm having my lunch, between Trimble and Lookout Mountains. Emerging from the gorge, the North River then turns its attention eastward and breaks through a gap between Lookout Mountain and Narrow Back Mountain at Stokesville. After leaving the Alleghenies, the tamed current languishes among the gentle fields and farms of the Shenandoah Valley until it joins the Shenandoah River near Grottoes.

* * *

A sudden spray of that same North River water snaps me out of map study as Toby uses a wet dog's prerogative to shake herself on the nearest person. She gets a couple of dog biscuits and the rest of my peanut butter sandwich for her efforts, reinforcing the behavior.

The calm surface of an upstream pool sparkles where water striders go about whatever it is that keeps water striders busy. The constant rasp of cicadas in the trees and the trickle of water slipping from pool to pool between rock crevices lull me. Toby goes back to the serious work of probing the riverbank for dangerous frogs and lizards. A high-pitched bird song almost beyond the range of my hearing is the only other sound.

For me, lunchtime is often the best part of a hike. A reward for making the effort to tie up loose ends at home, gather one's stuff and travel some distance to explore a new trail or become reacquainted with an old one. A chance to review collected treasures, consult field guides, read good nature writing and make some sense of a place. A time to think. And not to think.

Today's trip was the carrot on a stick that kept me glued to my PC to meet a week's writing goal. I picked this trail because it is beautiful and because it's just an hour's drive from home. And, on a weekday, I just might have this trail to myself. Told myself after my word count hit 5,000, Toby and I could dash over for the day.

Every morning, I'd sit myself down at white screen before dawn. Keyboard clicking, I made faltering progress. Click on Alt-T for Tools, W for Word Count. 1,009. Click, clickety-click and peek again. 2,228 . . . 2,785 . . . 3,140 . . . 3,355. The count edged up, sputtered, then stalled out at about 4,100.

Visions of crystal-clear water, sun-dappled river bottom, scurrying crayfish and glistening salamanders came between would-be writer and computer screen. Ah, to feel the cool air sinking down the hollow from Shenandoah Mountain, smell the soft, mossy earth of the forest. I yearned to float face down over an icy swimming hole and see my shadow on the bottom.

The targeted word count remained elusive. Physical activity became more necessity than indulgence. So. Refinement of goals was in order. My desk chair and I were going to need surgical detachment if I didn't take action. After all, these mountains have their magic. The pressures and mental detritus of the home office always fall away like discarded skin as I leave the sunny parking area and enter deep woods. The cathedral quiet in the dim light beneath hundred-year-old hemlocks and tulip poplars is balm to the senses. Invariably, I wonder why I don't do this more often.

* * *

On my picnic rock, I begin the examination of my small collection. The stones I chose simply for their smooth feel in my hand

and for their color. One rounded pebble has the grayish cast of the predominant sandstone here. According to the geology map, the sandstone of the North River Gorge is in the Pocono formation— a Mississippian rock derived from decaying animal and plant life during the age of amphibians, which began 345 million years ago.

lady's slipper, trillium, jack-in-the-pulpit

I have no idea what 345 million years means. In Earth time, with a life span measured in billions rather than millions of years, it's not much. At the time, fishes were plentiful and the first air-breathing amphibians were crawling out of swampy shallow seas that overwashed the area.

Another stone, also worn smooth by time and the river, has the reddish brown of faded cordovan leather. It matches the description of even more ancient Hampshire sandstone exposed farther up the gorge. Those sedimentary remains of the Devonian age, or age of fishes, were laid down some 400 million years ago.

The third rock is a piece of shale with the same reddish hue, but the colors are brighter. The sharp edges suggest this stone has not been tumbled long by the waters that swirl about my ankles.

Recent research for a book required that I immerse myself in geology. Starting out, I had little aptitude and even less interest. Rocks.

Cold, inanimate rocks. Dumb as a rock. Lifeless. Rock-hard. These were the associations I brought to the project. They were born of ignorance.

Rocks, it turns out, are made of life stuff. Created over dizzying time spans by unimaginable forces. When the life forms that made up these North River Gorge rocks were abundant, the landscape looked much different than it does now. The entire chain of the Southern and Central Appalachians was but a gleam in the eyes of Laurussia and Gondwana, two giant land masses preparing to collide and do a bit of mountain building. Once these ancient continents smashed together—a head-on train wreck in extreme slow motion—the layered sediments formed over previous millennia from decaying plants and animals were crunched, folded, twisted, turned cockeyed and thrust up into the air, possibly to heights that would rival today's Himalayas. Fossils of decayed marine animals from the Paleozoic Era ended up lodged in rocks high up the sides of North River Gorge.

River bedrock, exposed today like the jutting backbone of some monstrous dinosaur, also reveals the violent past. In the lower end of the gorge, the rock strata tilt upriver. Farther up the trail, long ridges of bedrock lean back the opposite direction, pointing downriver.

What's left of those once soaring peaks, like the sandstone of North River Gorge, is the harder material, the last to erode away. No wonder these soft blanket folds of western Virginia draw us as iron dust to a magnet. These rumpled remnants of once heroic heights contain the Rosetta stone that unlocks Earth's history.

Turning over the reddish rock in my hand, I wonder. Where's a geologist when you need one? In the presence of an earth scientist, this piece of shaley earth history would be giving up its secrets, accounting for its black pockmarks, the pink fissures, the scooped-out side. Spilling the beans. A regular raconteur. Do wizened geologists still get goose bumps handling material from such an ancient time? Can they go rock hopping across a mountain stream with carefree abandon? Or is each careful step a wondrous slippery link with the mysteries of the ages?

* * *

The jawbone I collected on the riverbank is about the size of a raccoon's. Four fairly worn teeth are intact. Already the bone is pitted and bleached, well on the way to contributing its substance to the next mountain-building event.

I look at the rocks and bone anchoring the geology map. Every hike up this orange-blazed path assumes a character of its own. Today, it's geology. Last month, Gina and I were into stream life and wildflowers. We turned over stones to find salamanders and crayfish. Checked the shell markings on freshwater mussels. Admired the flashy colors of a young northern water snake and an even flashier pileated woodpecker. Located the wilted remains of spring-blooming lady's slippers, Solomon's seal, trillium and jack-in-the-pulpit. On another trek up the hollow, my attention was drawn to an abandoned railroad bed, which provides easy walking where it coincides with the trail, and to the unusual absence of trash—a fact most assuredly due to the efforts of Girl Scouts who have a camp nearby.

Virginia's national forest lands are like that. Leave you feeling like someone on a short lunch break at an all-you-can-eat buffet. So much to take in, so little time. One sweet trail like the North River Gorge Trail has endless interest. Rocks with incredible earth history. Human history. Streamside wildflowers. Ferns that catch a ray of sunlight slanting through the leafy canopy high above. Deep, clear pool, built by beavers, holding a single trout suspended a foot below the surface. Riverbank tracks left by thirsty bobcat, black bear, white-tailed deer, white-footed mouse, gray fox.

Around every bend, another masterpiece. Nature's paintings, changing, moving, flowing in real life and real time with rippling stream, lush river grasses, glowing cardinal flowers, gangly joe-pye weed, blue mountain backdrop.

But North River Gorge, though extraordinary, is not unlike hundreds of other wild haunts in some two million acres of the George

Washington and Jefferson National Forests, most of which lie in the
western part of Virginia. Countless trails lead to countless waterfalls,
lakes, bogs, heath thickets, rocky outcrops, even old-growth forests
and wilderness.

In the early 1900s, these same lands were deeply wounded, torn
and battered. Stripped of massive virgin timber. Farmed out and abandoned. Badly eroded and in need of rescue. Alarmed conservationists—Gifford Pinchot, John Muir and Teddy Roosevelt among them—
worked to bring these ruined lands under federal protection. Luckily
for Virginians, our state got a generous share of the bounty. Despite
some parenting mistakes, just enough years have passed for nature to
make tentative strides toward healing those wounds.

* * *

I lie back on the sun-warmed Mississippian river rock. Toby comes
and goes. With my eyes closed, sounds take precedence. A breeze
riffles the leaves of nearby trees. Maple. I don't even have to look to
recognize it. Never knew I could tell a maple by its sound, but I can
squint one eye open and confirm what my ears knew they heard. Maple.

Not only do I recognize the sound, but I know immediately why a
flood of emotions comes with it. I remember the child I was when
three large maples shaded the house and front yard. In the middle was
a red maple, flanked by sugar maples on each side. My second-story
bedroom window was at eye level with robins' nests in spring. Gangs
of raucous blue jays gave noisy voice to fall. I positioned my bed
against the open window so I could put my pillow on the windowsill,
and it almost felt as if I were sleeping in the boughs of the maples.
More than once, I awoke with rain on my face or snow in my hair.

The trees remained with me through the seasons, whispering in
childhood dreams, drying and clattering through each fall. So accus-
tomed did the child become to the song of the maples that even
today, thirty-some years after I last had my head in that window, the

flood of associations from just the sound of their fluttering leaves is visceral.

Maple-edged memories retreat to the background as I open my eyes. In the patch of sky between mountain ridges, a red-tailed hawk catches a thermal, circling, rising, shrinking to a pinhead. Sky the color of a bluebird's egg. I am lifted with the hawk.

Actually, I understand that I could be equally content in hundreds of such mountain refuges. For today, it's quite enough to be on this slab of river rock under this particular patch of blue sky.

Tonight I won't hear the rustle of maples or the sighing of tall hemlocks and white pines, though life in North River Gorge will go on as it has through the centuries. The stream will tumble over boulders, swirl in eddies below alders, witch hazels and sycamores, pause at the trout pool to reflect a dark sky full of stars, and roll on down to the Shenandoah.

The next high water will sweep away my collection of rocks and bone, almost as if I had never been here. The difference, I suppose, is not the footprints I leave on the banks of North River, but the imprint North River leaves on me.

So why, I ask as I lick chocolate icing from plastic wrap, do I wait so long to come back?

Deane Winegar is a nature writer and wildlife photographer who lives in the Blue Ridge near Waynesboro with Shenandoah National Park bears for neighbors. She and her husband Garvey have written two guidebooks, *Highroad Guide to the Virginia Mountains* and *Natural Wonders of Virginia: A Guide to Parks, Preserves, and Wild Places*.

SEASONS OF LIFE
False Cape and Back Bay

Paul Clancy

Close on the heels of a late summer heat wave, a cold front races in from the west, surrounding us briefly with violence and beauty. Thunder and lightning, wind and rain, cool air and vivid colors. The wind clocks around to the northeast, hinting crisply of fall. And suddenly, as if on cue, a river of songbirds begins arriving at Back Bay National Wildlife Refuge and False Cape State Park. The low-lying persimmons and hackberries are alive with chirping and fluttering as hundreds of warblers, vireos, wrens and thrushes comb their branches for insects and larvae. The seasons have changed and a new cycle of life begins at the state's southeastern coast.

Because our lives seem to run in a straight line from childhood on, and years appear to start and end, we lose sight of cycles. Cycles of the sun, of the moon, of the seasons, of the earth, of life. But walk or bicycle on the interior roads of Back Bay or False Cape, hike along the oceanfront connecting both places, or canoe from one to the other. Or get there anyway you can and just sit. Take a deep breath and smell the pine needles and watch for the latest arrival by land or sea or air. This procession of life, from hawks and warblers in fall to ducks and geese in winter to shorebirds and osprey in spring, speaks of eternal rhythms, not of the calendar but of life itself.

For me, there are few better places to see and feel this than at Back
Bay, a refuge created specifically for the protection of migrating birds,
and False Cape, the adjoining state park that contains one of the last
maritime forests on the East Coast. They're part of the same narrow
barrier spit that is both wonderfully inviting and wisely inaccessible.

Just after the cold front muscles its way across the coast and out to
sea, Gary Williamson, the chief ranger at False Cape, hosts a bird
walk and I'm the only one to show up. What luck! It's just after dawn
on a cool September morning. First, along the walkway just out from
the visitor center at Back Bay, we check the arrivals. In an hour, we
spot a dozen species of warblers, vireos and orioles. There, pretend-
ing to be a nuthatch, a black-and-white warbler runs nervously up
and down the trunk of a persimmon tree, harvesting bugs. A yellow-
breasted, red-capped palm warbler feeds on the ground, hopping and
bobbing its tail. Now, a white tail band flashes in a persimmon branch,
a sure sign of a magnolia warbler. In the background, the wichety-
wichety-wichety call of a Carolina wren. Now, in the thicket, with
nice white eye rings, a yellow-breasted chat. And, strutting on the
ground like a miniature sandpiper, a northern waterthrush, yellow-
breasted, with brown brush marks.

These twittering, flitting songbirds have been on the move for
weeks, whether navigating by stars at night, Earth's magnetic field or
simply the coastline. The route by now is pretty well defined, a neck-
lace of wildlife preserves along the Atlantic Flyway. When fuel runs
low, they must stop and fatten up for the next leg, and the preserves
are the only places now that allow this to happen. Whether mosquitoes or midges, moth larvae or inchworms, they stay just ahead of the
cold snaps that threaten their source of food. Their odysseys can take
them from the Arctic Circle to South America. At the same time, a
shadow migration of swift predators like sharp-shinned hawks and
merlins takes place. They feed on the songbirds. Whither goeth breakfast and dinner goeth they. Fair enough. But the little guys wouldn't
have a chance without places to forage, rest and hide.

Meanwhile, on Back Bay and its interior ponds, a different part of the cycle is turning. Gadwalls and widgeons and teals, both blue- and green-winged, are pouring in. Fortunately, human visitors are scarce by now—the teals are skittish and appreciate the isolation. Winter's visitors, hordes of snow geese, tundra swans and Canada geese, will soon be arriving. Already, an advance party of snow geese has taken

snow goose

up residence. When the main contingent makes its appearance here and at Mackay Island Wildlife Area at the south end of the bay, the sky can seem blotted out by their silhouettes.

A winter image: The western sky over the bay is pink at sunrise. In response to some disturbance, there's a commotion near the shoreline and a great flight of tundra swans rises. With soft cries that sound like weeping and wingbeats like paper fans, they soar overhead, the reflected flamingo dawn on their breasts, then bank around to their gathering spot out of sight on the bay. Like the other wintering waterfowl, they're resting and gathering strength for the next cycle, spring's migration to breeding and nesting grounds to the north. Maximum fuel power is needed, so even slight human disturbances that cause unnecessary takeoffs and landings like this reduce the chances they'll survive the return trip. Luckily for them, interior trails are closed during winter months, with human traffic permitted only on the beach. That's when the place becomes a true refuge.

The refuge's eight thousand acres stretch along the coast and now, thanks to continuing appropriations, have begun gradually expanding to the bay's western edge. Along with the acquisitions, better farming practices are helping restore what was increasingly becoming a lifeless bay. The best signs are diving ducks and, along the shoreline, at least two bald eagle nests to which the builders return each spring.

The cycles at Back Bay National Wildlife Refuge are aided by intense management. Summer's mud flats, rich in organic material for shorebirds, are flooded in fall to make way for ducks. The grasses favored by snow geese are disked to expose their roots for feeding. Native seed plants like sunflowers, millet and bulrushes, greatly favored by dabblers and divers, are encouraged by manipulating water levels. With natural habitat missing in so many areas, these human activities help improve the chances of survival for hundreds of thousands of migrants.

I tread lightly. In winter months, quietly.

In the spring, these visitors will answer a different call and head north just as their replacements arrive: sanderlings, plovers, stilts, willets and their ilk, all skittish as teens on their first date. As the ponds dry, insects will deposit their larvae in the mud and the wading birds and newly arrived shorebirds will gorge on them.

It's about three miles along the beach from the Back Bay Visitor Center to False Cape, then another mile to the ranger station. I've made the trip by canoe, on foot in winter and, at low tide on hard-packed sand, by bicycle. This September day there's barely a soul on the beach. It's just a few miles from one of the largest population centers in Virginia, but you'd never guess. Several types of terns, including royal, orange-billed and Caspian, stand shoulder-to-shoulder, facing into the wind. There's even a species of gull from England, a lesser black-backed, that apparently got shoved off course by the recent storm and ended up here.

A pelican is fishing offshore and, just beyond, sun catches the shimmer of leaping fish as bottlenose dolphins strike. Spring's neonates are finding their hunting form, churning the water as their victims attempt to flee. As long as the near-shore ocean stays relatively warm and the food supply good, the dolphins will linger, then head down the coast, probably no farther than the waters warmed by the Gulf Stream near Cape Hatteras. Their winter replacements just off the Virginia coast: juvenile humpback and fin whales that apparently break away from southward-migrating pods—they're not yet interested in courtship and mating in the Caribbean—and feed off the bounty of fish pouring from the mouth of the Chesapeake Bay.

At False Cape, there are new signs of fall: foxes that make their homes in secondary dunes near the ocean now have thicker, browner coats than they did in summer. They frequently race out to the beach and grab fast-moving ghost crabs. Deer have now discarded red coats in favor of winter gray. Some leaves are already tinged with red and at dusk extravagant sunsets are the rule. At night, nesting horned owls add their magic as they call to each other. They've begun nesting, timing their breeding to match the seasons. By mid- to late-February, owlets will be in the nest and, a few months later, ready for spring's unsuspecting prey: squirrels, rodents, snakes, birds, a stray tomcat or two.

False Cape State Park is geographically much like Back Bay, 4,321 acres of land bridge connecting southeast Virginia to North Carolina's Outer Banks. A mile wide, six miles long. But in sharp contrast to Back Bay, the park has been left pretty much the way the first explorers found it. Sand from the ocean side gradually washes over to the bay and the land migrates slowly west, encroaching on what is still a vast inland sea. Until 1933, there were settlements of fishing and hunting families in a place called Wash Woods, but then a hurricane leveled everything. The hurricane of 1998, although much less damaging, uprooted trees whose rings attest to the sixty-five years of growth. The latest storm, fortunately, did little to what has become prime habitat for fall migrants.

False Cape was apparently named by mariners who were fooled by shoals that once gave it the appearance of the capes marking the entrance to the Chesapeake Bay. Now, as it nearly always has been, it is an isolated spit, an isthmus where nature takes its course. If you can get here and stay warm—important considerations before starting out—you can camp or hike year-round.

There are wonderful walks along the spine of the park, through cool maritime forests or along the beach. Or, as I love to do, simply hiking across from the canoe landing on the bay to the ocean.

Out on the bay, an osprey banks sharply as it flies over the vast inland sea. It seems tireless in its hunt, preparing to dive, then recalculating and circling again. The bay is ruffled by the wind and ripples gurgle as they reach the dock. Close by, a pair of wild ponies that have ranged across the border from North Carolina now stand beside the marsh, grazing in a cloud of bugs, legs stomping, tails wagging, skin twitching. They seem to take no notice of me as I walk by. Beside small lagoons, baby frogs, plentiful here, plop into black water. Invisible bugs strike the ponds constantly. Pink swamp mallows and beauty berries add extravagant colors. Somewhere back in the reeds, although impossible to see, snakes are hatching; it's that time of year. Quickly, the trail leads from marsh to mature forest of maples and sweet gums. Then, after a slight rise, to live oaks and loblolly pines.

Here you could be in any forest, except that the wind, the nor'easter blowing off the ocean, murmurs through the pine needles like a spirit. Leaves from the oaks, killed prematurely by salt spray from the hurricane, fly across the path. The sprayed and baked leaves seem as if they've been stunned by a blight, but the tough old trees will recover.

Beside the path, warblers are chattering in the woods and a woodpecker is hammering. In the pines, the dark aroma of fallen needles and vegetation is whiskey-like, intoxicating. There's a thicket of tangled vines, and mosquitoes, not yet done in by frost, are biting. Good for the warblers, not for me. A monarch butterfly, also stopping on its southward migration, flutters by on the path. A spotted ladybug lands on my knuckle.

The progression moves to wax myrtle, bayberry and persimmon trees, although there are still live oaks, more hunkered down as the dune line approaches. In a few places, wild grapes that taste like sour jam cling to the low trees. The bayberry leaves are as pungent as tobacco. As the dunes begin, a few maritime shrubs remain. The inner dunes are pockmarked by holes that are probably entrances to fox dens. At last the path falls down from the dunes to the wide beach.

Gulls are standing, facing into the wind, but terns are fishing in the middle surf. And farther out, again, a half dozen dorsal fins break the surface.

This is not a season for dying, not here. In a way, with the extravagant appearance of berries and nuts—food for the season's latest visitors—it is a new spring.

Soon, the warblers and vireos, thrushes and their many cousins, tugged again by instinct or dreams, take wing in Venezuela or Costa Rica and come our way again, this time full of song.

Paul Clancy lives in Norfolk, Virginia. He writes about nature, from swamp to sea, crustaceans to cetaceans, for the *Virginian-Pilot*.

THE FOREST RETURNS
Bottom Creek Gorge

Jim Crawford

On a rare warm day in February 1997, I hiked into the Bottom Creek Gorge Preserve, searching for the past. The preserve's trails, still covered with ice and snow in the shaded areas, the ground moist and soft underfoot from the winter melt, took me through fields and woods just beginning to wake from winter's chill. The majestic rhododendron thickets, thriving along the creeks and wet spring seeps, showed small pale green buds at the tips of their waxy leafed limbs. Other buds were just beginning their spring ritual. From a distant field, the faint red hue of the buds consorted with others in the woods to cast a rosy hint of rebirth in the oblique sunlight of lengthening days.

Underground, sap was moving, bulbs were responding to the light and heat of this warm day. I wouldn't see evidence of this activity for months, but under the ice-heaved ground a regeneration was underway. The preserve looked raw and scrappy in its winter coat. Through the bare limbs of trees I could see the ravages of past ice storms and the hurricane of a decade past. The forest floor was covered with downed limbs and trees.

Along with this natural pruning, the young woods showed years of persistent logging. The land had the imprint of human activity. Outcroppings of rock exposed old field clearings and springs. A weathered gatepost, its hinges frozen in rust, stood like a lone sentinel by the wide trail. Scattered around the preserve were several decaying homesteads, their roofs gone and the log walls sagging toward the ground.

Who left these marks? How long ago did they live here? What did they do? Questions like these kindled my exploration of the cultural landscape of the preserve and man's interconnectedness with nature.

＊ ＊ ＊

Bottom Creek Gorge Preserve, one of The Nature Conservancy's most visited preserves, is a place of edges, boundaries, isolation and awesome elevation changes. The 1,657-acre preserve, cloistered atop Poor Mountain just south of the Roanoke Valley, hugs the western edge of the Blue Ridge. Its foundation of Precambrian granite and gneiss is among Virginia's oldest geologic formations.

On this land a community grew up, faded and disappeared. The history of Bottom Creek, hinted at by the scattered remains still visible around the preserve, illustrates the story of many isolated mountain communities of the 1800s and early 1900s in the Appalachians. Altitude was a barometer of impoverishment. The higher you lived above the surrounding valleys, the poorer you were likely to be.

In the early 1800s, the heirs of General Andrew Lewis, who owned several hundred thousand acres of the highland plateau, sold off large tracts to settlers. Others moved into the area as homesteaders or tenant farmers. In the mid-1840s, among the homesteaders to the area was William Craighead. He came to Bottom Creek from nearby Franklin County with his oxen, his wagons, his tobacco seed, his family and an unknown number of slaves.

He acquired much of the land that is now the preserve by the early 1850s. The Bottom Creek community grew to around seventy people in its heyday from 1900 to 1920. There were two small stores, a one-room school and a church within the community. Two gristmills operated along Bottom Creek, grinding wheat, buckwheat and corn. Some farmers found they could make a living growing apples and there were many orchards throughout the area.

Marriages among the few families served to form strong bonds within the nearly self-sufficient community. Families tended to be large and the farms were divided or new land acquired for the next generation to farm. Registering land deeds, marriages and deaths required a day-long trek down the mountain, past Allegheny Springs and Shawsville and up Christiansburg Mountain to the courthouse in Christiansburg. As time progressed, the community's isolation from the rest of the county gained in significance. Montgomery County graded only a short distance of the road into the community once a year. The dirt wagon road down the mountain to Shawsville was steep and impassable during rainy periods. None of the roads in the community were ever paved.

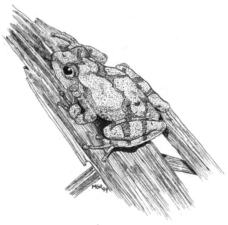

spring peeper

Within a few generations resources on the mountain were diminished and work became harder to find. With the advent of the automobile, increased mobility lifted the veil of isolation. Families left the community, drawn to jobs and better educational opportunities.

As the community's population declined in the 1930s, the county closed the school. Children had to walk several miles to catch a bus to attend Bent Mountain School in Roanoke County. Losing the school signaled the end of the community. Soon the stores closed. The community's slow demise concluded in the 1950s.

Isolation and the lack of county services depressed property values even after the community faded. A Roanoke doctor bought some property and used one of the old homes as a hunting lodge. Some of the fields were fenced and cleared for a cattle operation whose workers were rumored to manufacture a little moonshine now and then.

This isolation, provided by the mountain and the county boundary, allowed nature the time to renew, and adapt. The forest returned, covering bare hillsides, aged orchards, home sites and yards. Then one day in 1988, The Nature Conservancy's sign was erected on the land: Bottom Creek Gorge Preserve.

* * *

Today, many of those born in the Bottom Creek community and their descendants live nearby on the mountain plateau or in the valley around Salem and Roanoke, close to their roots.

To listen to the stories of people who grew up on Bottom Creek is to bear witness to the interconnection of man and nature. I met ninety-eight-year-old Virginia Kreger at her home in Roanoke. Virginia was born at Bottom Creek in 1900. A spry, petite woman, she still attends church and loves company. Her memories danced across her face as she recalled the joys of childhood games, church socials and close bonds established in circumstances where one's ability to improvise and make the most of everything was appreciated by everyone. Salted into these memories were those that echo sweat and sacrifice. She seemed to harbor no grudges, though sometimes the sadness that a little girl can feel was revealed in her laughter. This was a laughter in the face of hardship, born of a strong and feisty will to survive and softened by time. "They had hard times, they was the happiest times," she said.

Bottom Creek, the heart of the old community, forms the head-waters of the Roanoke River. From its inception along the ridges and springs of Poor Mountain, the stream meanders through highland plateau meadows and picturesque farmlands. Its clear water eddies and pools within banks of grass, shrubs and trees, and riffles over cobbles, sand and boulders in its golden brown streambed. Its tribu-taries and compatriots in this bucolic scene are Mill Creek, Big Laurel Creek and Little Laurel Creek, whose names give some clue of the area's natural and human geography.

Bottom Creek's waters provided food, recreation and power for the community, as well as a place of reflection. In 1850, Montgomery County granted William Craighead permission to construct a fifteen-foot-high dam to power a gristmill near the present entrance to the preserve.

The community church baptized its members in the sanctifying waters of the creek. One December day, Virginia Kreger and eighteen others were baptized in its frigid waters. The creek was frozen over and a hole was chopped in the ice with an axe. She remembers coming out of the water shimmering "like a leaf."

At the entrance to the preserve, Bottom Creek gains momentum. In the next two miles, it tumbles some seven hundred feet through Bottom Creek Gorge in a raucous series of cascades and pools. The creekbed is carved into smooth hunkering boulders and sandy alcoves composed of forest-green rhododendron groves, hemlocks and towering hardwoods clinging to the steep sides of the gorge. Cool mists from the falling water shimmer the leaves of sturdy plants able to keep rooted in this perilous zone. Butterflies dance above the eddies.

Midway through the gorge, Camp Creek falls two hundred feet into Bottom Creek, forming the second-highest waterfall in Virginia. Camp Creek's source lies nearby along the watershed divide between waters flowing to the Gulf of Mexico or the Atlantic Ocean.

The deep gorge etched into the flanks of Poor Mountain over hundreds of thousands of years provides pockets of unique plant habitat. Along the gorge's steep south-facing slope is a small shale barren of loose scree. This hot, dry biome supports the globally rare chestnut lipfern, whose closest relatives thrive in the southwestern deserts of the United States and Mexico. The north side of the gorge, out of reach of a century of logging, protects a stand of old-growth hemlock. Within this stand rises a species uncommon to this area, the Carolina hemlock.

The early community survived on a forest economy. The forest supplied many of life's necessities: shelter, fences, wagons, buckets, eating utensils, food, furniture, herbal remedies, heat and money, to name a few.

The steep gorge harbored some of the last trees harvested, tucked in its wild folds. Millard Collins, who left Bottom Creek in 1949 at the age of fifteen, told how he and his sisters cut oak trees in the spring "way down in the gorge." The teenagers stripped the bark from the felled trees in four-foot sections and hauled the bundled bark by hand up to where they could hoist it onto a horse-drawn sled. The horse pulled the loaded sled up to their father's truck to be sold at the tannery in Salem.

The community's children and teenagers played on the mountain and down in the gorge with abandon. "We'd get on them old grape-vine swings over on the sides of them mountains," Millard recalls. "Of course we fished a lot, too. If the gnats were biting real bad, that's when we'd go to catfishing, you know them little madtoms about that long," he says, holding his fingers five inches apart. "You could catch them just as fast as you'd throw your hook in the water. We'd take them up and put them in the spring race and they'd live till we'd eat them all and then we'd go back and get some more."

Today the creek provides habitat for three rare species of fish endemic to these waters: the orangefin madtom, bigeye jumprock and riverweed darter. A host of micro invertebrates can be found in its stream bed. I have netted caddis-fly larvae, hellgrammites, mayfly nymphs, gilled snails, stonefly nymphs, water pennies and other water creatures indicative of an ecologically healthy stream.

One early spring day Genny Craighead Henderson, a great-great-granddaughter of William Craighead, showed me her birthplace on the preserve. It rests in a swale at the western edge of a field, surrounded by encroaching woods. An old roadbed passes to the south of the house, curving around the hill and into the woods beyond. The ground sloping out of the field, moist from spring seeps, seems to cascade down the grade into the woods. The house itself is gray and silent, its weathered siding and faltering tin roof slowly recycling to the earth. Rusted pieces of metal are scattered among clumps of grass and brush around the house under a canopy of pioneering trees.

Genny tried to convey how this place used to be, the life and beauty that reside in her memories. It was a difficult process. Nature and time have transformed the physical backdrop of these memories. I tried to imagine the sounds of young children playing, the muffled talk of young boys walking along the road in the twilight to visit sweethearts, to feel the solitude and grace of the picket fence, the dahlias, the chickens and kittens roaming the yard, the slosh of water carried from the springhouse and the clatter and buzz of a young man's industry in the mill across the way.

Genny showed me a faded black-and-white photograph of herself at the age of five standing in the yard in front of a picket fence. Her left hand, thumb forward, is propped on her hip, the elbow stuck out smartly. She has a slight grin under her steady eyes. Behind her in the distance, a shed stands on the cleared, rocky hillside.

Lowering the photograph, I looked around. The barren hillside and the yard have returned to forest. I turned, but no matter how I tried to align myself with that grainy image and its story, the shed, the garage, the granary, the cherry trees, the pear trees, the picket fence around the garden, the wash kettle, all were gone. Instead, I was confronted with time and change.

* * *

Last spring, the first reunion of the Bottom Creek community was held at the preserve. It had been nearly fifty years since the last remaining resident, Bob Hall, died. Millard Collins and Genny Craighead Henderson were the reunion's main organizers. Others helped, including volunteers from The Nature Conservancy.

The morning of the reunion was dark and threatening rain. By noon the sky cleared, as if by blessing, to a sunny day. Family members numbering in the hundreds gathered in the field near the Funk Cemetery. Awnings covered tables groaning with fine home cooking. The air seemed charged as the older folks visited, looked at old photographs and reminisced. Their young grandchildren and great-grandchildren played amongst the chairs and tables and in the beds of pickup trucks, oblivious to the significance of this gathering. Handshakes, hugs and laughter accented the hum of conversation around clusters of lawn chairs. One card table held a box of fresh homegrown cantaloupes complete with a good knife so folks could help themselves.

For many the reunion was a cathartic event, a healing of the past. Some had not returned to this land since they had left many years ago, still unable to forget the hard times they had on this mountain. One woman told me her husband wouldn't come to the reunion. "Why would I want to go see that mountain that kept me from getting an education?" he had asked her.

My wife and I were invited. From my explorations, I had recently self-published a book about the cultural landscape of Bottom Creek. The day was a montage of new and now-familiar faces. The stories of their past, so intimately interwoven with this land, took center stage. We were in a field of memories.

The words of a former resident echoed the sentiments of many Bottom Creek residents, reflecting the dual essence of this preserve as a refuge of nature and a repository of their history. "That was the best thing," he said. "Now I know can't nothing be happening over there."

For several months after the reunion I received calls from former residents wanting a copy of my book. I hand delivered the books whenever possible, taking the opportunity to meet more Bottom Creek folks and listen to their histories of Bottom Creek.

One evening, Mavis and Leymond DeWeese from Elliston called. Now in their seventies, they are part of the Bottom Creek extended family. Over the phone we agreed to meet halfway at the market on Main Street in Salem.

I was waiting on the sidewalk when they pulled to a stop beside me. Leaning into their open car window in the summer night air, I listened to Mavis tell stories that are core to her life experience: farming corn, the little church, the mountain. Leymond smoked a cigarette and grinned, glancing away, out the open driver's-side window, as if the universe and all that mattered was quietly there with him, sitting behind the wheel of his blue '86 Thunderbird, framed by the window and the darkened Main Street backdrop. His hand was like many I have shaken in the last year, leathery, wrinkled and strong as a plow.

It has been a year and a half since I started exploring the cultural landscape of Bottom Creek. An early fall chill settles in the nooks and crannies of the preserve. Alone, I walk the trails accompanied by stories I've heard and memories of people I now know, bestowing a sense of wonder at the continuity of this place through layers of time, decay and growth.

I am reminded of my own sense of place, my roots. I am drawn to the mystery around each ridge and bend of these mountains, as if my eddying spirit might settle and fill its creek-traced bottom like an early mist.

I pass the rotting post standing beside the trail I'd seen so long ago. Three rusted brown strap hinges still clinging to the post are all that is left to hold the memory of a gate. The crisp sunlight highlights the Virginia creeper climbing the lichen-splotched post. I imagine brothers Zean and Bob Hall halting their wagon, the sound of the gate opening, the wagon creaking forward a bit, then the gate closing

and the wagon rolling on to the rhythm of the mule's steady clop—
the rhythm of time.

Exploring Zean Hall's homestead, remarkably still standing
amongst the trees like a ghost in the woods, I discover his springhouse.
The grinning face of Millard Collins flashes in my memory. I remember him telling me the story of how he carried a five-gallon bucket
full of spring peepers he had dug from the bog at his family's place on
the other side of the preserve, and deposited them below this previ-
ously peeper-less springhouse. "That little frog in the spring makes
so much noise that you can't even sleep," Millard said, still fond of his
childhood prank. Next spring I'll see if the descendants of those
peepers are still here.

Now, though downed limbs and brush clutter the springhead, water
still flows from the rocks laid long ago to form the spring box. I photograph this stonework, feeling the satisfaction the stonelayer must have
felt to live by such a robust spring on the flanks of Poor Mountain.

Near the entrance to the preserve, two stately spruce trees bear
silent witness to a home site which sheltered many families over the
life of the community. Leland and Lula Craighead lived there as young
newlyweds. Lula's hands planted and nursed the spruce trees and some
of her flowers around the house still appear each spring. Here children changed into dry clothes after swims and visiting preachers stayed
during one- or two-week revivals at Bottom Creek Church. The sounds
of a cappella hymns caressed these spruce trees as do the perched
crow's call and the mockingbird's chatter today.

The sounds of children playing have long since faded. I can hear
the whisper of the mountain breeze and the gurgle of the spring that
quenched many parched throats of those who worked this land.

The land holds these memories erect through time. The early fall
sun strokes the earth, cutting through the green canopy, illuminating
the hundred standing fieldstones in the Funk Cemetery, marking the
last remains of unidentified souls who lived out their lives on this
mountaintop. The earth sags at their feet. A grove of sassafras trees

has taken root and now their sturdy, furrowed, gray trunks appear to offer the cantered slabs a vertical reference. A breeze stirs the understory while the stones seem still. It will take the accumulated frames of many human generations to capture their gradual repose to earth.

Jim Crawford is a cultural geographer and musician. "The Forest Returns" is an additional vantage to his longer, self-published study, *Bottom Creek: The Cultural Landscape of a Mountain Community*. He is currently researching the tobacco culture of Southside Virginia for a PBS documentary, *The Legacy of the Bright Leaf*. He lives in Roanoke, Virginia.

The Nature Conservancy acquired the 1,657-acre Bottom Creek Gorge Preserve beginning in 1988 and also holds a 920-acre conservation easement on the headwaters of Bottom Creek.

A River Good Enough:

On the Merits of Modest Water
Moormans River

Donovan Webster

At its highest reaches, the Moormans River is pure, national-anthem stuff. Trickling off the east side of the Blue Ridge summit, springing from billion-year-old rock near the Skyline Drive, it begins as a seep too shallow to support much life—but it's spectacular nonetheless. For the next mile downstream or so, the tall, steady line of Afton Mountain stands behind you like a protective older brother, while, to the east, the voluptuous roll of Virginia Piedmont stretches edibly green toward the Chesapeake Bay. Standing up there and staring, you know exactly why the original settlers chose to stay around.

Then, as the creek meets its first feeder tributary and drops into a draw, fish start to take up residence. Shaded by mountains for all but the highest daylight hours, the upper Moormans is a place of hardwoods and lichen-painted rocks, where stair-step waterfalls drop into knee-deep pools the size of suburban carports. This is the domain of tiny brook trout, ferocious little natives who'll pounce on drowned summertime dry flies—even in a sifting snow—like kids on a bowl of Cap'n Crunch.

The fish hit like this for a reason. Up high, where rains tinged by hydrocarbon exhaust and the makeup of the riverbed's stone itself turn the water a little acid, there's not much to eat. And as the stream's course is still pretty vertical and fast, a hungry trout has to strike quickly at a passing meal—or it's moved along downstream.

Hooked and brought to hand, these high-country brookies barely span my palm. They're beautiful and plentiful. And despite my fairly strict Protestant upbringing, it's satisfying to find the fishing so easy. But it isn't the ease that draws me to the upper Moormans (and anyway, it's not that cushy: you still need to walk uphill an hour to get to it). Instead, it's the trout themselves. Despite—or maybe because of—their tiny size, they feel solid and cold in my fingers. They're hard and shiny, like jewels: their bellies pale sunset orange; the leading edges of their green pectoral fins lined by a creamy white band. Their minuscule ribs are visible beneath thin sheets of fine, olive-colored scales, and—rising above that—each fish's flanks are pointillized with genetically-unique starburst dots in orange and blue; the spots morphing across their smooth backs into a crazy vermiform: black and pale green stripes—like a jumble of Appalachian ridgelines—worming over their tops to leave them almost invisible from above.

Between the fish and the scenery, after spending a morning on the upper Moormans—working to outsmart the only trout species never lauded for its intelligence—I always return home relaxed and energized, as if I've been away for days. Somehow, in puruit of those little fish, the dust kicked up by life at lower altitudes settles out. I've gotten my ticket punched, and I don't recall ever leaving there in anything close to a bad mood. At my house, in fact, there's a standing joke between my wife and me after a Moormans trip. It goes:

Janet: "How was the fishing?"

Me: "Nice. I got six or seven twenty-four-inchers . . . in four- to six-inch portions."

From your home water, you could do far worse than that.

✳ ✳ ✳

When traveling and writing about the world is your business—as it is for me—you've got to be careful if you fall in love with a place. You find a landscape that really speaks to you, that encapsulates all still good in life and on earth, and your impulse is to tell everybody. So you write it up and publish it in a magazine (or for a book like this) and then—somewhat miraculously—you return to find the spot you loved has become crowded. Overnight it's filled with cars and humans (a few of whom you discover instant aesthetic differences with), and the place loses some of whatever made it so killer to begin with.

eastern brook trout

You can rationalize most of this away. It's snobbish and elitist to keep these spots to yourself. And it's your job to tell people about new places, right? If you're a writer, that's what you're exchanging: new stories for grocery money. But if—for a paycheck and a few attaboys from readers—you're also selling a place out, well, occasionally the process leaves you a little sick for what's been traded.

I should know. I've wrecked my share of places.

In the 1980s, my brother and I found the little town of Cameron, Montana, and for a few years it was our playground. A hundred miles north of Yellowstone Park and hard along the trouty banks of the Madison River, Cameron's population numbered six. It had a mercantile that also pumped gas, a real U.S. post office, and a few rental cabins behind an amazing bar/restaurant, the Blue Moon Saloon, where the jukebox took only half-dollars, stuffed game hung on the walls, the cat slept on the pool table, and Jesse—the bartender—served up hot coffee in the morning and icy beers and monumentally large and messy cheeseburgers the rest of the day.

Then the dam began to crack. We told a few people. They told a few more. When the number of Cameron insiders reached a sort of critical mass, I wrote up the Blue Moon Saloon in *Outside* magazine, figuring "What the hell can it hurt?"

A year later I had my answer. Cameron had its own fly shop (in a new, clean, high-tech, log-cabin-style building), and the formerly unpeopled saloon's parking area was thick with shiny four-wheel-drives. Inside, the bar had been commandeered by Wall Street types drinking Gibsons, and my old pal Jesse had hied back to his native Hawaii, having seen his broad, golden, empty valley turned into a full-on tourist destination.

I tell this story not to brag about an anointed existence (as with all adult choices, there are trade-offs to a writing career—trust me), but to illustrate that sometimes you should work to love places that aren't so perfect they break your heart in the end. Because places do change. Always will. It's like hot neighborhoods in big cities: part of their energy comes from the waves of people and businesses washing over them. There's an allure to all that—and it makes those spots fine for short visits, though a little unstable if you're up for a longer stay. If you settle there, don't be surprised if your neighbors change semiannually and that tiny restaurant you love either crashes and burns or is purchased and "upgraded" by a chef whose skills at the burner aren't as tight.

Which is why I chose to live near the Moormans. I wanted a less-showy neighborhood for my home water: a river I could fish, explore, and boat a little when conditions were right, but which wasn't too good. I only wanted a river good enough. And, so far, it's proved just right. There are better trout streams in the area—the Rapidan just a few miles north, spring-fed Mossy Creek over the mountain near the Shenandoah Valley town of Weyer's Cave, and the permit-only water inside the Wintergreen resort to the south—so most people don't even bother with the Moormans.

Its relative inaccessibility doesn't hurt, either. To get to the Moormans it's a long drive up Sugar Hollow's narrow entry track; and then, if you want to catch fish that aren't imbecile hatchery rainbows planted downstream in the cold months by Trout Unlimited, you have to park where a cable gates off a fire road to the Shenandoah National Park and hike upstream. That's a little too much work for most people. Which is just the way I'd hoped.

A number of years ago, back when my wife and I were living in a brownstone in Chicago's Lincoln Park, we spent close to a year trying to decide where to raise our brood. We couldn't find a city that gave us enough in schools and value, and most of the semirural places we liked had their own sets of educational problems—not to mention few had the airport my work demands. Finally, after months of dithering, I admitted to Janet I really didn't care where we lived so much, provided it had four things: a house our kids would have trouble outgrowing, good schools, a passable (but not too nifty) trout stream nearby, and a serviceable local airport.

We limited our searches to a few places, and set off—checkbook ready—in earnest. Then one night, as I was tying shut a reporting assignment in Utah, a fax arrived at my hotel room. It had a blank line running along its bottom. It was a purchase agreement for a house, and I was to sign it and send it back. Janet had bought a place outside Charlottesville, Virginia. We'd visited there a few times while home-foraging in the past, and I knew the Moormans was nearby, that the schools were good, and that the airport had three different airline connections.

"So, uh, you really like this one?" I asked when I phoned Janet, about a minute after reading the price tag.

"I do. I really, really do," she said. "It's what we wanted. It's set back off the road, up on a hill. It has a huge screened porch and a big woods off behind and a little stream down in the woods and pastures after that. You have to come see it. You'll love it."

I ordered a drink from room service, wrote my name at the bottom of the fax, and sent it back. What else was there to do?

* * *

As a neighborhood for fishing, the Moormans has proved better than most. For a few years, the fishing was spectacular closest to the ends of the March to December season. Summer was—and remains— slow: with the river's flow so low, you have to sneak up on each pool, hiding behind the jagged rocks at the outflow and then, with glacially paced patience and the lightest possible touch, drop your fly in. At that time of year, you start by fishing each pool's out run, so as not to spook the fish nearer its head—which invariably happens anyway. Then, each successive cast reaches farther toward the pool's top until eventually you're making long, reaching casts toward the mostly dry waterfall at each pool's front, the fly dropping to the river's surface at the edge of what foam is still splashing down in the summer's near drought.

If you're a counter, you won't bother with the Moormans in summer. That's how slim the pickings are. At that time of year, you have to take satisfaction other ways. By August, if I fish halfway up a hole and don't put the pool's trout down, I call it a success. And if I catch my share, well, then I don't feel so guilty when I drop by Garrison's Grocery in the little town of Whitehall to drink a mid-afternoon beer. (Stopping by Garrison's on my way off the mountain is yet another reason to hang out at the Moormans: it's one of those utilitarian rural stores that rents videos, sells everything from sidemeat bacon to nails to fresh garden vegetables [in season] to blaze-orange hunter's caps, and also functions as the local post office.)

As home water, the Moormans is also pretty quiet. Except for the rare University of Virginia student hiking with a significant other or doing fieldwork, it's unusual if I encounter anyone on my trips. For a while, on Wednesday mornings in spring, I used to see a retired gentleman who drove up from Richmond. While he freely admitted having spent his career as a tobacco company lawyer, he was still nice enough. And a few times toward the last, we'd actually sit down on adjoining rocks and share lunches of smashed sandwiches and bruised apples pulled from our fishing vests.

Then, in the spring of 1995, I noticed the old man wasn't fishing the river's higher reaches like he once had. He was staying low, usually below where the fire road fords the river for the fifth time inside the park. About the third morning I saw him, I also noticed his arms and legs had grown thin and sticklike, and then over lunch one day he admitted he'd "spent a lot of last winter sick."

Soon after that, the man's son began to fish with him. The son—in his mid-forties, probably—was an agreeable enough guy, too, though his clothes gave him away as a visitor to Richmond. He wore hip waders pulled up only to the knees of his Lee jeans, and a cowboy's rodeo belt, and a red "Wyoming Lariat Company" gimme cap. Finally, after a little probing, he told me he actually lived in Sheridan, but was home "visiting for a while."

Then the river's flow dropped and I didn't see the old guy or his son anymore. I've not seen them since, and have generated two explanations for this. One has to do with human mortality—the old man died—and the other with God.

In 1995, two other things happened to the Moormans. The first was that in the water I fish—above the dammed impoundment of Sugar Hollow Reservoir—the trout season was opened to year-round fishing. The state fisheries department was experimenting with a few rivers, to see what winter fishing would do to wild trout populations, and I was a little worried—though I shouldn't have been. It was a fairly cold winter, and even I rarely fished the upper Moormans. And besides, as I've mentioned, God had another plan.

In June of 1995—as the spring's fast fishing was settling toward another summer of stealthy, low-water trout stalking—a series of storms dumped twenty-some inches of rain on the Blue Ridge in a pair of days. Then it rained steadily for another week. The resulting flood scoured out the Moormans bed, fish, boulders and holding pools, its vegetation . . . everything. The dam at Sugar Hollow was about to be undermined and had to be opened, which washed everything downstream for miles, too: the collected trout and river rocks and silt and downed trees poured over the dam's spillways, picked up speed, and tore up bridges, driveways, and the gravel and paved sections of the roads for a dozen miles below Sugar Hollow.

By August, as the roads opened again, I was back into the river's highest portions to explore, but I was there without a fishing rod. The fish were gone, flooded away. Which is the other reason I think I've never seen that old man again—he had better sense than to fish where there was nothing to catch. But, as I say, I was up there looking around without a fishing rod. In my left hand I was carrying my nine-month-old daughter; in my right, I was clutching the little fist of my two-year-old son. I'd just returned from five weeks in Mongolia—where I'd been researching a story on fossil hunting—so to give Janet some sorely deserved free time, the kids and I examined the newly widened and shattered riverbed, often returning home wet from the process.

With the flood having widened the river—saplings and mature trees alike were wrapped around trunks of larger specimens downstream—the Moormans course had been rendered wide and sunny. It was hot, so flirting with and eventually ending up in the creek became something of a necessity—not to mention the peak of every visit's dramatic curve. This began a tradition of what my kids now call "trips to the national forest."

We'd wade in some of the shallower stretches left by the flooding; seeing a few snakes, and—in what scant pools were left—a few inch-long brook trout who'd survived by burrowing between rocks. We found a feeder-creek moraine with a kid-size, algae-coated sliding rock between shallow pools. Even the baby liked that.

We began to bring my wife. She liked it so much she began to bring a basket with sandwiches and Cokes and a blanket to sit on. Countless dozens of days are now whiled away up there, most of which culminate with a stop at Garrison's on the way home. The kids get juice. If the day's hot enough, I still get a beer (which has been known to make Janet frown). The rains from Hurricane Fran in 1996 did some further damage to the river, but nothing like the '95 floods. And slowly, over the last couple of years, my family and I have watched the animals along the Moormans return. We've seen otters, deer, eagles, snakes, and crawfish, and even—after a few days of thawing rain at the end of one January—a black bear who looked cold and wet and was standing alone in a pane of weak sunlight trying to warm up.

Up high, the Moormans is a different river now. Wider and sunnier. The fish still aren't back in the numbers they used to be, prompting the wizards at state wildlife to begin stocking it with hatchery-bred brook trout—which has done zip to boost populations. Because of these interlopers, there's less room and food for the stream-bred trout, and very few hatchery fish are hearty enough to survive for long in such a demanding environment. But, then, what the hell. As a friend of mine—a private-practice stream doctor and consulting fisheries biologist for the state of Montana—once told me: "If a stream can't support stream-bred fish, it's screwed anyway. Not even a state biologist can make it worse, and the only tool that'll fix it is time."

Fortunately, I'm noticing more overwintering natives with every passing year, so time must be unkinking things. A few of the toughest hatchery fish may also be selecting in, and if you add to that the few original natives who managed to weather the floods of '95 and '96, it's only a matter of years until the upper Moormans returns to its former glory. In the meantime, I fish it anyway. It's my home water, after all. And because of the wider channel, I now get a better suntan.

* * *

A few words about stocker trout. Earlier in this essay, I made de-
meaning reference to Trout Unlimited's practice of stocking the
Moormans below Sugar Hollow Reservoir with hatchery rainbows.
And—just maybe—I was a bit harsh. After all, I do support Trout
Unlimited, if only for the way they keep an eye on general trout populations and corresponding environments. To that end, I buy the twenty-
dollar pass to fish the Moormans Trout Unlimited–stocked, fly-fish-
ing-only water each year. And for precisely one day annually, I do park
my car at one of the Trout Unlimited–sanctioned turnouts downstream
of Sugar Hollow to pursue, as my brother calls them, "tourist fish."

The day I do this is unvarying: the last Sunday in January, better
known to the world as Super Bowl Sunday. On this, every year's most
overhyped day of manufactured fun and commercialized excess, my
friend Ed and I have turned a trip to the middle Moormans into a
parallel tradition. After a few years of watching, we've learned that
the stocking truck stops by every Friday from late December to February, and by Sunday the fish are acclimated enough to their new
home to generate a little appetite.

Trout Unlimited (TU) sure spends some money. The trout they
slop into the Moormans are big—silver as nickels and slab sided.
Many weigh two to three pounds. And as I not-so-nicely alluded to
earlier, they're fretfully easy to stick a hook into. Just drag a fly through
the pools below the reservoir's dam—those long, smooth holes with
cobble bottoms seem to hold the most fish—and BAM! Nothing
more to it.

To catch these fish, I've always had success with the hairiest, most
obscene-looking flies in my box: woolly worms or Tellicos. You stand
on the bank—or ankle-deep in the stream if you really feel like tapping into nature—and begin to cast. Once. Twice. A third time. Within
minutes you'll be landing large trout. Exactly like the ones you see
cleaned and bedded on chipped ice at Kroger. Like their gutted breth-

ren at the fish counter, you'll notice many of the Moormans stocker fish have battered lower tail fins and nubs where their pectoral fins should be—a telltale (and unfortunate) by-product of living one's life in the concrete raceway of a trout hatchery.

Don't believe me? Take a look at those hatchery trout next time you're in the grocery. Fins that've spent a lifetime fluttering against concrete eventually wear away. (Oh, and incidentally, completely silver isn't the natural color for rainbow trout. If they're living on a diet the Lord intended—insects and crayfish and minnows—their shoulders are often deep olive or twilight blue, speckled with black spots, with streaks of bright crimson topped by a slash of black along their flanks and gill plates. The first time you lift a wild rainbow from a river, its coloration can knock you clear ashore.)

Fitting with accepted trouter's religion, the Moormans TU stretch is catch and release—until May, that is. By then, either spring flooding has pushed all the stocker fish a few dozen miles downstream into the Rivanna Reservoir (which I've never fished but drive past regularly on my way to the airport), or the river grows so warm and its flow plummets so low TU deems it more humane to let people take and eat the fish than doom what few remain to suffocation and slow boiling in the river's summer-warmed climes.

Therefore it is resolved: for one Sunday each year, I toss aside prejudice and stop by the middle Moormans to stand near a few hearty trouters (Ed sometimes among them) to pursue the sportsman's equivalent of veal. If you can get past the pointlessness of it, it's a fun couple of hours. Those big, fat, simple fish fit nicely with the broad excess of the day. And it's nice to get out a little before the game; to build the illusion of having done something healthy before hoovering down chips, salsa, guacamole, pretzels, cheese, seven-layer salad, grilled steak, fried potatoes, sundaes for dessert, and a halftime show so grandiose and flabby it makes even that meal seem sleek.

Of course, I also recall spending one pre–Super Bowl visit walking in the woods behind the river, because the stream was so crowded I didn't see the value of one more guy in there, terrorizing the fish.

So I left my stuff in the truck and took a walk. For an hour that afternoon I watched a pair of pileated woodpeckers strip the bark off an enormous—and recently deceased—standing pine. Behind them was a tall granite cliff, and I sat on a rock and took in the scene with a kind of calm awe, as if it were a movie. The speed with which those large, prehistoric-seeming birds worked—the precision of it—made the Moormans simu-trout and the fishermen chasing them look even sillier. If I shut my eyes I can still see those birds in the afternoon, their bright red, crested, diamond-shaped heads and long necks moving, bobbing and weaving from side to side, pecking strongly forward, dark dagger beaks driving below the bark and sometimes sending it falling in sheets, like house painters scraping off exterior latex. Rotten wood showered the forest's floor. It sounded like rain.

* * *

I've probably gone on too much about the Moormans flooding. And I've made it sound like a bad thing. Which—if you're a boater—it isn't.

Each spring, I count myself among the few who wait for the Moormans to flood. And some years (unfortunately for those who live along its shores) the floods arrive. Snow melts, the heavens rain, and the Moormans starts to rise. Then—in the time it takes an unwatched hound to snatch a steak off the kitchen counter—small groups of kayakers and canoeists slip in and play on the fast, now-pregnant river. Known as steep creeking or flood paddling, this sport can be a somewhat dangerous calling, but its rewards—in terms of nonstop action and challenge—render the gamble worth it for a few of the area's more cavalier paddlers.

I put in just downstream from the town of Whitehall, at a narrow concrete bridge on the state road north out of town. By then the river has flowed ten or so miles from its source, far enough downstream that—if a flood has raised the water level—you can safely slip in a kayak or whitewater canoe (leave that old aluminum job on the pond at home) and go. I've made several of these trips, but, to give an idea of just how much fun a flood on the Moormans can be, there's one story that stands out. It was a Friday in early March, that spring's first really nice day: cloudless sky, air temperature in the seventies. I'd been watching the river for days, driving up every afternoon to monitor its rise. After a drizzly week, its level was perfect.

I'd coerced Ed, a freshly minted doctor, away from the errands and responsibilities he always had on his day off. (The convincing, actually, proved easy—that's how nice the afternoon was.) I've known Ed nearly half my life, since the second or third year of college, and throughout the intervening years—while he was a pilot in the Navy and through med school—the mortar of our relationship has been these relatively spontaneous adventures. Even seventeen years ago, we'd regularly bust away from studies to explore new places—from farmlands to cities to Mennonite and Amish towns—in the interest of, like bears going over mountains, seeing what we could see. Even now, though the passing time has put achy muscles and a few adult obstacles in our path, seeking fun on a sunny afternoon is still seen by both of us as a top-drawer way to spend a few hours.

So there we were. Standing below the concrete bridge on Virginia's State Road 810, loading our gear into Ed's two-man whitewater canoe. We pushed off a little after three o'clock, me in the bow. The river was still very high—and fast—but its mud-stained brown of the past few days had settled out. Whirling panes of clear water spun and slid beneath us until, with a few paddle strokes, we pulled even. After slipping through a few small rapids, we came to a large five- or six-foot cascade that dropped, changing direction, through two switchback turns. Backpaddling above the drop, we eased into the first section, dug in with our paddles and cut back hard, moving fast now, hit a rock, and got knocked hard off balance. We'd started to right ourselves when the floodwater pushed us crazily, tossing us against a large boulder and hurling our canoe upside down into the falls' plunge pool.

The impact—both with the cold water and the creek's bed—was a painful shock. Pinned beneath the still-hurtling boat, I was raked across the bottom's bouldered contours, praying not to get smashed between the out-of-control boat and a rock. Where Ed was—and what he was up to—was not on my mind. After five or ten seconds underwater, I twisted my legs free and popped to the surface, one hand gripping the canoe's gunwale, wrestling with the boat as it hauled me downstream. Ed was behind me, clinging onto the stern line as if it were attached to a raging stallion. Waist deep in the roiling current, we finally got the canoe to shore, chased our paddles—which had floated a way downstream—emptied the boat, rehashed the wreck, took note of new bruises, and set off again.

I'm proud to say we flipped only once more while negotiating the dozens of rapids and falls ahead. At one point we even hit the roots of a partially submerged tree—head on—which illustrates one of the great dangers of paddling floods. Water flowing beneath semi-submerged objects makes for some colossally unpredictable pulls of current, which can trap a person and drown him with horrifying force and speed.

On that afternoon, though, we stayed blessedly out of trouble. Beneath the first warm sun of spring, the current slung us bobsled-style through turns and down long, drag-race straightaways. We passed prim dairy farms and tumbledown wood houses. The scenery moved at an amazing clip; everything from pastel green pastures to steep mountain chasms. During low-water summers, these places are off-limits thanks to trespass laws. Now, however, taking advantage of a short-lived flood, Ed and I passed by quickly, legally, and easily—having only to keep watch for obstacles, boulders, or floating logs that might capsize our boat.

Minutes spooled into an hour. Exhausted from the cold water, hard paddling, and nonstop concentration, we pulled against a large, flat rock and stepped out to warm in the sun. Pods of trout and suckers circled the pool above our rock. The limbs on the trees were getting that furry green covering—a sure sign Virginia springtime would soon explode.

The sun slid lower. The air began to cool. Ed, a wonderful guy—but someone who occasionally makes Gary Cooper seem like a nonstop talker—weighed in with a rare, unsolicited opinion: "Hell of a fine way to spend a Friday afternoon," he said, sitting on the still sun-warmed rock.

We got back into the canoe and paddled hard, the Moormans high water lifting us above what are usually gardens of rock, its liquid surplus smoothing all but the worst drops. Above a few of the larger falls we'd backpaddle upstream, buying strategizing time before heading in, the canoe's bow arcing into open air before we'd slice—with a drenching splash—into the pool below and out the hole's downstream side. Across the afternoon, herds of cattle were our only spectators.

Before long evening was upon us. We made one last, three-foot drop just before a bridge, then paddled the canoe ashore. We'd parked my station wagon nearby, to drive us back upstream to Ed's truck, which had a rack for the boat.

We stowed the canoe safely beneath the bridge and made for the car. Another adventure logged into memory. I fired up the ignition, cranking the car's heater on full blast. Before leaving, I turned for one more look at the river. Piano music drifted from the stereo. In the first of twilight's shade, the Moormans had gone dark and full as a ripe plum.

Donovan Webster, a former senior editor for *Outside* magazine, has written for the *New Yorker, National Geographic, Audubon, Smithsonian,* and the *New York Times Magazine.* His book, *Aftermath: The Remnants of War,* was recently published in paperback by Vintage. He lives with his very patient wife and children at the foot of Virginia's Blue Ridge Mountains.

I Write from a Mountain Farm
Clinch River

Richard Cartwright Austin

Several years ago on a fine June day, I wrote this entry in my journal: "Two blue herons swept in for a landing as I stepped onto the porch early this morning. They nest, I believe, in cliffs on the far side of the Clinch River, less than a mile away. In a few moments they arose, circled the small pond below our garden, and separated. One lighted near the pond in the top of a small box elder. The heron perched, immobile, like an exotic Christmas angel. The other came to rest on the bough of an ash tree across the hollow. It bent the bough beneath its weight, keeping the great bird in full view. I had been preparing breakfast while Anne studied in the living room. After interrupting each other several times to view the birds' movements, we decided to move our morning devotions to the porch swing. A fresh, wet breeze sprung up in anticipation of a summer shower. The great birds arose, joined in formation, flew down the hollow, across another pond, and away. Our devotional reading from the Gospel of Mark said this: 'Wherever Jesus put in an appearance, all who touched him got well.'"

* * *

I write from a steep farm overlooking the Clinch River as it meanders through the mountains of southwestern Virginia. Occasionally I write about the farm, but always I write from it. It is not simply that from the windows of my study in our secluded house halfway up a hollow on Chestnut Ridge, I look out upon wooded hillocks, ponds, and a garden. Like the trees, my writing seems to emerge from the soil of this place that made me welcome twenty-some years ago.

Before that I had been pastor to nine churches in the Big Coal River valley of West Virginia. There the strip mines were tearing down the mountains above the homes of us all. Responding to the distress of the people I served, I helped to organize a fight against strip mining that continued for five years until the day I stood near President Jimmy Carter in the Rose Garden while he signed the first federal law to regulate strip mining for coal. It was during that time, around the first Earth Day, that I heard a call to devote my ministry to discovering the connections between Christian faith and environmental responsibility.

So I came to southwestern Virginia to try farming with some friends, and I rented a house nearby. When I explored the hollows and ridges behind that house, I met a natural beauty that I had never before experienced. Then my landlord offered to sell the entire farm, and I bought it. I persuaded one of my nearby friends to marry me and join me in the farmhouse. That was twenty-three years ago.

I read the Bible over again from cover to cover. So many things jumped out at me that I had not noticed before—such as the fact that the choir of those who praise God includes all creatures. My neighbors began to show me how to farm, for I had never done this before. Some of the techniques they taught me I appreciated, some I questioned. There were many choices: how to till, where to clear, whether to use fertilizers and chemicals, whether to obtain a tractor or a team of horses to help me.

I made a lot of mistakes those first years, but I learned something important: the best choice would nearly always yield a beautiful result, while poor choices left ugliness in their wake. Increasingly, when

I made farming decisions, I leaned on my aesthetic sensibility. As I
began to farm I read a new book about my favorite theologian, the
Puritan preacher and philosopher, Jonathan Edwards. I saw clearly
that the experience of beauty was the fulcrum of Jonathan Edwards's
philosophical system. This insight illumined my own engagement with
beauty on Chestnut Ridge. I began to add philosophical and moral
depth to my intuitive, day-to-day decision making concerning farming, forestry, and animal husbandry.

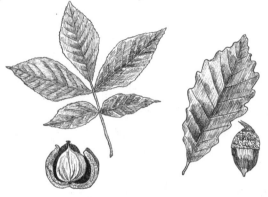

shagbark hickory and chestnut oak

It took ten years for this interplay of experience with reflection to
ferment into an "Environmental Theology," as I would name it. During these early years I was making maple syrup on the farm, growing
commercial strawberries, and tending a garden. At last the strands of
practice and reflection came together in a complex moral, philosophical, and practical insight, and I was seized with the urge to write.
From the soil of this engagement on Chestnut Ridge, four books
emerged: a biblical study, *Hope for the Land*, a study of nature spirituality, *Baptized into Wilderness*, a philosophy of ecological relationships, *The
Beauty of the Lord*, and a book on environmental ethics and public policy,
Reclaiming America. These books are not about Chestnut Ridge Farm in
a narrow sense, but they came from this soil—just as much a product
of the farm as my crops.

After my books were published, I was invited to teach theology students and began to speak more frequently across the United States. Yet my dialogue with Chestnut Ridge Farm continued to deepen. From my experience farming with draft horses, I was drawn into national discussions on the ethics of human relations to animals. Out of my concern to manage my hardwood forest in an aesthetic, productive, and responsible manner, I have begun to work with The Nature Conservancy and other organizations on schemes to develop an infrastructure for selective, sustainable forestry—an alternative to the prevailing cut-and-pillage practices. Because my farm has an allotment for tobacco, I have joined with others to design regional alternatives to tobacco farming that will protect the economic utility and the cultural integrity of small farms. Because I farm small patches using organic principles, I must constantly reflect on the boundaries between the cultivated and the wild, seeking farming techniques that keep the cultivated healthy and the wild free.

I am mortal, and some days I feel my age. It is not enough to farm well this year. I must plan future protections for the community of life on Chestnut Ridge. The Nature Conservancy and I have designed a conservation easement to assure that my successors also treat this land with respect. As soon as the protective easement was in place, I donated a portion of the farm to The Nature Conservancy to serve as a homestead for some beginning farm family who might not otherwise be able to afford land of their own. As I near retirement age I write more and farm less.

Recently, when a backhoe was working on the farm, I asked the operator to dig two fresh graves in an old ridgetop cemetery, and then fill them in again. Anne and I know that this earth is where, someday, we want to be laid to rest. Since we would prefer that our children and our friends do the job, not some undertaker, we want the graves to open easily. On a healthy farm, life and death and new life flow forward continually.

Beauty, I have learned, is discovered in relationships. The most beautiful person is the one whom I love most deeply. The most beautiful place is the place I tend. God is supremely beautiful when we experience God's love.

A place, a landscape, will become beautiful for us as we embrace it with insight and empathy. If you have any doubt about that, you should watch researchers from The Nature Conservancy joyfully reach through the muck on the bottom of the Clinch River to check on endangered mussels.

In my book *Baptized into Wilderness* I wrote about John Muir, the first human to understand the California Yosemite scientifically, and the first person of European heritage to love it with a consuming passion. It was John Muir who persuaded Teddy Roosevelt to protect Yosemite as a national park. I tried to imagine what Muir's perception and devotion meant to the beloved, to the Yosemite Valley itself.

Muir saw the beauty of Yosemite directly, as an engaged human observer, and he also experienced it indirectly, through complex ecological intuitions. Imaginatively entering the experience of the Douglas squirrel among the trees, the water ouzel in the rushing rapids, and the mountain sheep among the peaks, Muir sought to see the environment through their eyes and to share their delight.

We know that some species have sensory capacities that humans lack. Similarly, with his reflective capacities, Muir could experience the relationships of the Douglas squirrel in ways the squirrel itself could not. Muir could see ecologically and historically, and he could be analytical; but he never allowed analysis to distance him from those with whom he shared that space.

The distinctive quality of John Muir's presence enriched the Yosemite landscape. He showed how humans might relate to wilderness with integrity, benefiting both nature and the human participants. As he heard the rocks and rejoiced with the waters, he brought the glacial past and present experience together in a climax of meaning. Yosemite was never more beautiful than when John Muir leapt its peaks and gazed upon it with love and delight.

Would it not be wonderful, on the day of final judgment, to be told, "Your farm was never more beautiful than when you were there, growing with it."

Richard Cartwright Austin, Environmental Theologian with the Presbyterian Church (USA), writes from his farm near Dungannon, Virginia.

In 1998 The Nature Conservancy received a conservation easement from Richard Cartwright Austin and Anne Leibig on their 159-acre Clinch River farm and woodlands.

To Love a Place
Cross Mountain

Chris Bolgiano

I have learned to watch for the occasional day on Cross Mountain when nature shows her most murderous face. It happens only every few years. The last flare of autumn in fallen leaves is first extinguished by sodden winter. Then temperature and moisture may conspire with evil intent. The dark hump of mountain through my western window turns deathly pale in a fine mist. Raindrops gather at the ends of bare twigs, to freeze into blades of ice. Ice dulls the green of the cedars to the color of doom. Sometimes the air is still and suffocating. Sometimes there are gusts of wind like tracer bullets across the forest floor, tossing up helpless leaves. If I ventured out unprepared, Cross Mountain would kill me with hypothermia in a few hours. On such days, I feel most deeply my love for this place.

Although I lack personal experience with motherhood, I suspect this feeling is akin to the love of a mother for her serial-killer child. It is an unconditional, unreasoning, undeniable love. Its power takes me by surprise. I am disarmed, but I am not, after all, rendered so witless that I want to go outside today. Instead, with the requisite cup of home-grown herb tea, I sit at the window, savoring the ironies of emotion and environment by watching to the west.

For the last fifteen years, since my husband and I moved here, Cross Mountain has filled my western horizon. It rises at the edge of the Shoemaker River Valley, west of the much wider Shenandoah Valley. In the pattern that defines land ownership throughout much of the southern Appalachians, the rich valley bottomlands are held in private ownership, and national forest starts about halfway up the thin-soiled slopes. My hundred-acre tract on the flank of Cross Mountain is on the ragged private fringe, and our back border adjoins the George Washington National Forest. That puts us on the threshold of more than a million acres of undeveloped, forest-covered public land, which is itself more or less connected to another six million acres of national forests and parks along the spine of the mountains.

bobcats

I sit with arms hooked over the back of a chair at the window, alert for any activity in the gloomy light outside. Small creatures have fled, seeking cover in cedar trees and under brush piles, but two deer come to lap up spilled corn from the squirrel feeder. They stand quietly with heads down. It's snowing now, and the white flakes on their dusky backs turn them once again into spotted fawns. They roam my land and the government's, not recognizing the difference. For the last fifteen years, I've followed their example, trying to understand Cross Mountain as a whole.

There was little in my early years to lead me toward a life immersed in nature; I was a child of cities and suburbs. But as it happened, I came of age during the Back to the Land Movement in the counterculture 1960s. It was a blessed time. I'm proud to be an aging hippie, weaned on the slogan of Peace and Love, man. I took seriously the idea that serenity and wisdom could most surely be found in an earthbound life. For a double dose of nature appreciation, I married a biologist. We moved to a small farm, but soon realized that what we were looking for lived not in the fields, but in the fencerows. Those weedy, overgrown borders between pastures were home to wild things. It was wild nature we craved. So we sold the farm and moved to the woods, into that mysterious forest world at which the fencerows could only hint. Going back to the land came to mean, for me, going back to the forest.

The deer have disappeared. In the gashes made by old logging roads across the slopes of Cross Mountain, snow is collecting white and soft, like the buzzard down that Indians used to stuff into wounds. Like the pioneers that replaced the Indians, I am not native here. Like them, I left family history behind. Genealogy has always seemed to me to be a pointless pursuit. My ancestors were either handsome or plain, smart or stupid, kind or cruel. Or, if they were like most people who ever lived, they were all of these at various stages of their lives.

I have no ancestors buried on Cross Mountain, their bones to become part of the trees and the deer. Instead of human stories, I look for tales the land has to tell. Cross Mountain is my textbook. Some of its oldest pages are the creek rocks, and if I scan carefully I can pick out those that are scored in small circles by shells of lives lived three hundred million years ago. The evolutionary heritage of life in the Appalachians is profoundly ancient, yet most of the signs I see are fleeting. A cluster of wind-thrown trees in Mushroom Flat records a storm a decade ago, if my measure of moss on the root mass is accurate. Half a millennium and the pits will be mostly filled in, the roots well rotted. Charred logs in Finite Hollow are pages of billowing smoke, blistering fire. Inscribed maybe eighty years ago, in a few hundred they'll be illegible. A muddy streamside is a blackboard, scribbled by passing feet and erased by every rain. When snow falls, the forest is a white sheet embossed with animal tracks. I follow them, burying my mind in a vision of their creator, remembering myself only when I turn and face my own footprints.

Today is not a good tracking day because the snow is too blotchy for my eye to decipher any imprints. Even with binoculars here at the window, I can't detect the tracks of the two deer that just left. Maybe they've gone up to the little plateau where a cluster of tall pitch and Virginia pines might give them some protection against the snow. Unless the snow is very deep, branches catch most of it, leaving bare earth remaining in dark circles beneath pines, especially white pines. The little plateau seems an odd place for pines, because hardwoods generally outcompete them where slopes are moderate enough to hold soil and moisture.

The pines whisper a different kind of story, in which humans figure as the agent of change that has altered the original scheme of things. The moldering split-rail fence snaking straight up a steep slope, with locust trees (a sure sign of an old opening) growing only on one side of it, tells of hard human use. So do four acres of dense grape-vine draped over scrubby trees high on the east face of the mountain. All over the mountain, young chestnut trees struggle valiantly but vainly to beat an imported blight. Almost every single chestnut oak tree, a dominant species here, is actually one of four or five or even six stems all sprouted from a single cut stump. If you trace a circle by connecting the centers of each of these trunks, you get a close approximation of how large the original tree was. The sizes amaze me, and I look around trying to imagine how the forest once was.

There are a few scattered places on Cross Mountain where it's possible to find some echo of what used to be. Most trees are between seventy and ninety years old, an age we document by counting rings in the firewood we cut. Most trees fit easily within the embrace of my arms. The occasional individual or couple of trees that are bigger generally mark the corner of a land boundary, or the line of a former fence. On a ridge to the north, a rusted logging crane with iron wheels confirms the industrial nature of the lumbering that swept through all the mountains in the early twentieth century. So widespread and thorough was the destruction that the federal government bought up the land to stop the erosion and the wildfires. That's why we have those millions of acres of public land in the southern Appalachians.

Just south of my house, where a creek flows through an unusually wide bottomland, a decent depth of soil along the slender braided flow of the stream has created a tiny cove of a few acres. The trees here are no older than the surrounding trees, but they're larger because of the better soil and the protected site, down between two steep slopes. I can't quite reach around most of the trees. They're big enough to attract serious attention from pileated woodpeckers, as many oval holes attest. The undergrowth is subtly different from other areas, more layered. There's a lot of standing and down deadwood, including a lightning-split tree trunk I use for a bench. This structural complexity, apparently fostered by the better conditions in the cove, makes it the closest thing to an old-growth stand on this side of Cross Mountain. Along the top and down the steepest, rockiest draws, there are individual oaks that are not very large but are gnarled and twisted by age. These are the survivors, trees too poor or difficult of access to have been worth taking.

The mountain is shaped like a U, its ridgeline hovering around a modest elevation of about twenty-two hundred feet. Inside the U, in the heart of the drainage, I once found what appeared to me as the most beautiful creek in the world, bedrock stepping down in gray slate ledges, each filled with limpid pools in which many large fish swam. I've never found it since. Sometimes I wonder if it was magic, but Cross Mountain is not known for magic of any sort. Aside from the obvious fact that it does have a name, one that appears on

U.S. Forest Service maps at least by 1927, Cross Mountain is quite anonymous. It has no areas designated as special. Whatever ecological uniqueness it might once have harbored was presumably lost during the last, most devastating cycle of cutting. All the reports I read when we first bought land here—soil productivity assessments, wildlife habitat ratings, dependability of stream flows—ranked it fair to poor. The foresters we consulted all agreed that the trees were typical mixed Appalachian hardwoods. We should not expect anything beyond the ordinary on Cross Mountain.

But even after centuries of abuse, the forests of the southern Appalachians still rank as the most biologically diverse temperate woodlands in the world. There are mosses, fungi, salamanders, insects, mussels, fish and flowers like none other on earth. This abundance of living forms, and the unique communities they create, invest Appalachian forests with mysterious grandeur. Though they are only a green shadow of what they used to be, the woods of Cross Mountain are still so lovely they lull me into believing that anything is possible.

And it is: on Cross Mountain I have found such uncommon plants as fringe trees, round-leaved orchis, lily-leaved twayblade, red mulberry trees and one of the few cucumber magnolias I know of in this area. A blinking saw-whet owl one autumn afternoon earned me a county bird club first sighting record. Warblers rare for this area, like Wilson's and the orange-crowned, flit through. Ravens nest somewhere along the top of the mountain, and woodcocks have danced near its foot. Wood turtles appear occasionally, apparently expanding the southernmost extremity of their range. In addition to all the predictable varieties of small wildlife, I have found salamanders and snakes of mysterious species (at least to me). I have seen mink, bear and bobcat. Cross Mountain is a classic example of revelation, through time and conscious attendance, of hidden depths below the surface of understanding.

The surface of the ground outside is becoming glazed now, as the snow turns to sleet. If this keeps up all night, even the lowliest ground dwellers will have trouble finding their next meal. On such days as these, when Cross Mountain unleashes its deadliest powers, I recall to mind as an invocation its opposite mood, the glorious days of spring, when blue skies are mild and dogwood blossoms spangle white across the unfurling green of the forest. On those days I sit out on my deck to soak in the blessings of air and light, and to mind the mountain. I listen for the songs of migrating birds and watch the slopes and hollows that course down Cross Mountain to see what's going on, which is usually nothing obvious. It was on one of those days in our early years here that I first heard someone hot-rodding out on the dirt road, undoubtedly throwing beer cans as he went. The roar broke the forest stillness and voiced everything I feared in life, defiled everything I held sacred. My anger leapt until I cursed the driver with a vehemence that, afterward, astonished me. I found myself flushed with hatred. I understood then where all the anger in the world comes from, the intensity that lights wars. It comes from me.

There are other lessons I am learning from Cross Mountain. The cedar in front of the deck obstructs the panoramic view from my window, but once, after a deep snow had buried the forest floor for weeks, I saw bluebirds, robins and cedar waxwings, famished, search out the tree's blue-black berries. Having glimpsed the role of that single tree, I begin to sense the whole in the part, the universe in the atom. I see that the forest is like human society. Each tree is an individual, wounded by life in idiosyncratic ways, yet inextricably part of something larger than itself. When a tree dies it molders calmly to show how easy it is to return to earth, in the process that nurtures us all. With the forest as example I can fit myself into the inexorable cycle of life and death. It's the only way I *can* fit in. Without ancestry or progeny, I have no past in this land, and no future. I have only the present moment, the eternal present of forest life. Just at this moment a branch in the cedar tree is shedding its icy load in a cascade of razor-edged shards. I'm glad to be sitting here with steaming mug in hand, safe inside, where there is mint instead of murder in the air.

Chris Bolgiano writes on nature and travel for the *New York Times, Washington Post, Audubon, Wilderness,* and other publications. Her books include *Mountain Lion: An Unnatural History of Pumas and People* (1995) and *The Appalachian Forest, A Search for Roots and Renewal* (1998).

Prime Mountain Real Estate:
"Best Views in the World"
Shenandoah National Park

Eric Seaborg

> It just happens these mountains are made for a road, and everybody ought to have a chance to get the views from here. I think they're the greatest in the world, and I've been nearly everywhere in the world.
>
> —Herbert Hoover on the future Shenandoah National Park

Any well-traveled connoisseur of our grandest parks who has been overwhelmed by Yosemite's ineffable granite faces and giant sequoias, humbled by the geological rainbow of the Grand Canyon, or awestruck by the otherworldliness of a Yellowstone where you can catch a trout in one stream and boil it in the next, and who then admires the vista from Skyline Drive may well wonder: was Herbert Hoover as myopic about scenery as he was about economics?

Shenandoah's graceful mountain-hills are as lovely as so many of the Appalachians' folds, but what distinguishes them, what raises them to crown-jewel, national-park standards? They make up for any lack of jaw-dropping superlatives with the three choice attributes any realtor loves: location, location, location.

The entrance lies just eighty miles by interstate due west of the nation's capital. And fittingly, if not for a politically astute, tireless promoter with powerful connections, this stretch of peaks might have gained no more attention than the national forests to the west and south. George Freeman Pollock came as a teenager to inspect some land his family owned on the shoulder of Stony Man Mountain and loved it so much he contrived a way to cobble a living by developing a resort he called Skyland. At the end of the nineteenth century, you could leave Washington on the Friday night train and be in the mountains on Saturday morning, where Pollock promised: "The air of this altitude is fresh and pure, filled with ozone almost to intoxication, and grateful to the robust as well as the ailing."

The National Park Service hoped an eastern park's accessibility would increase the constituency for all national parks. Pollock played host and tour guide to the commission investigating sites for a southern Appalachian park, and conspired with the Byrd political machine, which coveted the financial returns of a national park.

The commission members had already found many proposed locations wanting, so they came to the capital's backyard with low expectations. But Pollock led them through the virgin hemlocks he had bought out from loggers to the six high cascades of White Oak Canyon, and the most skeptical commissioner summed up his reaction: "Well, I'll be damned."

For though these gentle mountains do not rise like the Rockies, they are not insignificant. If you follow the Appalachian Trail south from New England, after you leave Killington Peak in mid-Vermont, the next time you tread on a four-thousand-foot mountain is on Pollock's Stony Man.

"Our mountains," Thomas Jefferson wrote in *Notes on the State of Virginia*, "are not solitary and scattered confusedly over the face of the country; but . . . they commence at about 150 miles from the seacoast, are disposed in ridges one behind another, running nearly parallel . . . as they advance north-eastwardly."

The easternmost of these unconfused crests is called the Blue Ridge, a formation that stretches from Georgia into Pennsylvania. Shenandoah Park straddles the formation's northern last hurrah, before it melts into lower ridges in the mid-Atlantic states. (The park draws its name from the river and valley it overlooks to the west. These are not the Shenandoah Mountains, a long ridge that rims the valley's western side.)

The Blue Ridge is a thin line here, a scant barrier to the internal-combustion culture, which motors over interstate highways at each end of the park. But the ridgeline was the first barrier westward-migrating pioneers encountered, and the obstacle was great enough to muscle-powered culture that its east and west slopes were settled by different groups entirely.

The rolling Piedmont to the east was colonized by Thomas Jefferson and the Anglo-Tidewaterites. They crept away from the coast at the deliberate pace it took tobacco plantation society to exhaust the soil.

Shenandoah Valley people came from the north, founding towns contemporaneously with those on the eastern side. The first were Pennsylvania Dutch, followed by Scotch-Irish, traveling south along the Shenandoah River in search of sustainable family farms. Settlement funneled up the mountain valleys, where rivers cut paths of less resistance.

Even after roads finally crossed them, the mountains endured as a cultural divide. Fewer than one in ten Virginia slaves lived west of the Blue Ridge. To this day, you'll hear the phrase, "That's a Valley name."

As population grew on both sides of the mountains, those who didn't head west found land by moving to the hollows, gaps, and ridges. The forest they found here was good to them, dominated by the chestnut, a tree so useful that mountain culture became almost as entwined with it as the Plains Indians were with the buffalo. From the morning you were rocked in a chestnut cradle to the evening you were buried in a chestnut casket, every part of that tree provided shelter, food, and cash: logs to build your cabin, wood to burn, rails to fence in your livestock, nuts to eat, nuts to feed hogs, nuts to sell, shakes to put on your roof, shakes to sell, bark to sell to the tannery.

Then an Asian fungus wiped out the chestnut tree in a generation. A traveler in the 1920s described a two-square-mile area that "must at one time have been entirely a pure chestnut grove. Now every tree was dead. . . . The area was as free from tree growth as are some of the western plains. There were chestnuts of tremendous size—a foot or two or three feet in diameter."

Shenandoah salamander

In Hoover's time, the vistas from the ghost forests, mountaineers' fields, and loggers' clearcuts were so ubiquitous that photographs are almost unrecognizable compared with today's forest-carpeted mountainsides. Hoover built a presidential retreat on the best mountain trout stream he could find within a reasonable commute, and like Pollock before him, fell in love with the place.

It was Hoover who started moving earth for Skyline Drive, a great public works program completed by Franklin Delano Roosevelt's Civilian Conservation Corps. The drive became synonymous with the park, dominating its narrow elevation, and creating three distinct worlds that overlay and intermingle with each other, three conceptual Shenandoahs.

The first Shenandoah is the Skyline Shenandoah of the masses, the popular park of the Disney World non-culture, a 105-mile-long drive-thru. About two million people per year motor up to one of the four convenient Skyline Drive gates, handing over $10 ("You want fries with that?") for the right to pull off at the overlooks to inhale the McViews, engines running and stereos thumping, before scurrying on to the next point of interest. Like the new drive-thru funeral homes, there is no need to leave your car to pay your respects. In those expansive views you get the big picture; it's quality time with Mother Nature.

FDR said at the park's dedication: "In almost every other part of the country there is a similar need for recreational areas, for parkways which will give to men and women of moderate means the opportunity, the invigoration and the luxury of touring and camping amid scenes of great natural beauty like this." Trouble is, for too many, the parkway became the park. FDR based social security on a payroll tax so everyone would pay in and everyone would have a stake. The Skyline Drive lowest-common-denominator strategy is similar. The taxes of the masses support the park, and they get the easiest way to almost see it.

While I may whine about the Skyline Shenandoah, there's an argument that the more visitors the better, for it has immense potential as an educational tool because it is one immense display of the depredations of air pollution. Since 1948, the area's visibility has dropped by 60 percent, 80 percent during summer vacation season. Early visitors reported seeing the Washington Monument from the drive; historical view distances reached 70, even 125 miles. In 1991, the average view distance was less than 20 miles. Rangers tell stories of people turning back from the first overlook to ask for their money back on smoggy summer days when visibility did not extend even to the park border.

Sulfate and nitrate particulates purvey a grayish cast. Ozone is said to add a yellowish tinge. On summer evenings, the sun disappears behind impenetrable mauve strata well above the horizon, making the notion of watching a sunset seem quaintly old-fashioned. The Clean Air Act Amendments of 1990 exempted old power plants from installing pollution control equipment because they were expected to go out of commission. But the grandfather-exemption acted as a subsidy to power companies to keep senescent plants in operation. Visitors can see for themselves the effects of such policies—tighter standards may have prevented even greater deterioration in visibility, but have not improved it.

Tourists flock to Shenandoah because designating any acre as a national park is equivalent to hanging out an international flashing neon billboard: "Scenery Here." The washed masses have been conditioned to expect the best, crowding park roads in search of the "attractions."

In exchange for these belts of overused motorways (ironically called parkways), nature lovers and future generations obtain protection for the silent majority of acres: no logging, mining, or other "economic" uses. Step a quarter mile away from the Skyline Shenandoah and find the second Shenandoah, a transcendent, peaceful woodland for people desperate for a piece of nature. The second Shenandoah is for people who agree with Emerson: "In the woods, we return to reason and faith. There I feel that nothing can befall me in life, no disgrace, no calamity, which nature cannot repair."

Aldo Leopold might have scoffed at calling these cutover mountains a wilderness, which in his seminal proposal he described as a continuous stretch of country held in its natural state that was "big enough to absorb a two weeks' pack trip." In places, Shenandoah Park is too narrow to absorb a two-hour walk. You can reach any spot that strikes your fancy on a day hike, and yet Shenandoah is sought out by backpackers—it has the most crowded backcountry of all the major national parks, measured by the number of overnight visitors per acre.

Leopold also said: "I am glad I shall never be young without wild country to be young in. Of what avail are forty freedoms without a blank spot on the map?" For millions from Washington, Baltimore, Richmond, and more, Shenandoah is the closest, blankest spot on the map. The nearest place where they can, in John Muir's words, "Climb the mountains and get their glad tidings [where] nature's peace will flow into you as the sunshine into trees . . . while cares will drop off like autumn leaves." Presidents from Jefferson to Teddy Roosevelt have let their cares drop off here. Even Newt Gingrich joined the local trail club, although his system apparently rejected that graft before any environmental attachment could take hold.

But for the less environmentally challenged, presidents and plebeians alike, accessibility is critical to developing an attachment to the natural world. The second Shenandoah offered me the best wild country to be young in, where, as it did Pollock, nature drew me in to an attachment for this place.

On my earliest trips, nature was secondary to tramping the trails to the rocky viewpoints (without big rocks to look out from, mountains are just tilted forests), a backcountry version of the Skyline Shenandoah. But as Yogi Berra pointed out, "you can observe a lot by watching," and the more I observed, the more intriguing it all became. Nature has a way of tantalizing, from the first time I saw the electric flash of a goldfinch (a color I thought couldn't exist in a natural animal) to the unforgettable mating dance of the woodcock, a sight you will only see if you are in a meadow at twilight: the shorebird-shaped woodcock jumps into the sky, circles in a spiraling gyre as if picked up by a tornado, a hundred feet above the ground, higher, all the while emitting an odd twittering generated by the wind on its wings, until, as if the tornado suddenly dies, the bird plummets to within an instant of being dashed against the ground, when it spreads its wings for a fluttering parachutist's landing.

Mysteries endlessly drew me in—like the case of the sick horse whinnying in the woods. But horses do not live in the woods. This was not quite a horse's whinny, too small, too broken, too mobile, a mystery—how do you look up a sound in a book?—until one day I happened to glance into a copse of briars and locust trunks to see huge eyes staring fixedly back. I never knew owls came in extra small. The bird book said it was a screech owl, its voice "a tremulous, descending wail; soft purrs and trills." With that starting place, a bird-call tape confirmed the identification.

And now when I hear a screech owl it sounds nothing like a horse, but so exactly like a screech owl that I wonder how I ever compared it with a horse. I'd had to categorize in order to comprehend, to have organizing principles to learn. Nature can even teach lessons about yourself, a level deeper than the identity of an owl, to the heart of how your head perceives and processes knowledge.

It could be that every one of Shenandoah's three-hundred-plus vertebrates has a similar story to teach, all the way down to the almost luminescent little red efts that appear like earthworms crawling across roads on rainy spring days. Each salamander's world consists of only a few square yards of earth, but together they outweigh all the mammals and birds in this forest combined.

The park's only found-nowhere-else animal is the Shenandoah salamander, a species endemic to only three high-elevation spots. When the species was listed as endangered, it seemed to me that caring about some overspecialized loser so limited in imagination as to adapt to a few hundred acres was like worrying about a company that makes buggy whip handles going out of business. I changed my mind when I realized that salamanders are the Appalachians' answer to Darwin's finches. The ancestors of Darwin's finches were blown to the species-poor Galapagos, where they adapted to fill niches that on the mainland other species filled. Some act like woodpeckers; others have beaks "designed" to open certain seeds. The finches fill many roles in a limited geographic area, speciating to adapt to exacting niches. The salamanders' strategy is the inverse. They slowly spread over a huge geographic area, in a niche at the top of the leaf-litter food chain. Once spread out, limited mobility isolated certain groups, and their adaptations to exacting local conditions led to speciation. Darwin used the finches' speciation as evidence to prove his theory of evolution; the salamanders' adaptation is important to science in a similar way.

And that brings us to the third Shenandoah—the scientist's domain. Shenandoah was the first national park formed by purchasing land (the western parks were simply carved from the federal domain), and as such has been called the first attempt at creative rather than defensive conservation. The third, scientific Shenandoah is a 196,000-acre ecology laboratory, a grand experiment in regenerated wilderness.

The fauna's resurgence has been dramatic. One resident never saw a deer or bear during decades of living in a hollow that became part of the park. Rangers estimated the park contained two black bears when it opened; fifteen deer were re-introduced. Today, Shenandoah's population of three hundred or so black bears is the densest in the nation; white-tailed deer estimates are in the range of six thousand.

Roger Tory Peterson and James Fisher were struck by the forest's revival by the 1950s: "When the Shenandoah National Park . . . was established . . . some purists . . . claimed that the area did not measure up to National Park standards. It was mostly second-growth woodland, they said; there was relatively little primeval forest. . . .

"If the East is to have wilderness, it must restore it. The second growth, now thirty, forty, or fifty years old, which clothes the Shenandoahs, will, while our sons are alive, become trees eighty, ninety, or one hundred years old. Our grandsons may see a forest approaching its climax."

Now it appears that Peterson and Fisher may have spoken too soon. The forest's resilience is weakening in the face of unrelenting attacks. The very concept of climax forest may be obsolete here, replaced by a state of continual change. We've introduced to the natural world the same breakneck pace of technological change that drives our culture, infesting it with so many stresses that Shenandoah seems a place to study not natural but artificial ecology, nature's response to outside manipulation. Exotic competitive species, introduced pests, and pollution all place stresses on the native flora.

In the succession toward a climax forest, light-loving, fast-growing trees are the pioneers. Their very success at producing a canopy allows shade-tolerant trees to outcompete their offspring.

The native chestnut forest disappeared beginning in the 1900s; Peterson and Fisher saw maturing on the hillsides and ridges the replacement usually called oak-hickory forest, although in Shenandoah that meant perhaps seventy percent oak. The evolution of this young-by-succession-standards forest was interrupted by the gypsy moth's sweep southward. To gypsy caterpillars, oak is the filet mignon of the forest, and their appetites knew no bounds, entirely stripping some trees. Though a healthy tree should survive a single defoliation, thousands did not. The caterpillars left acres of bleaching skeletons, and new openings in the forest. What will fill these openings?

Perhaps the shade tolerators have already gained a foothold under the oaks and will continue to grow. Or maybe the exotics have changed the rules so much that it will look like some groves of "forest" along the section of the Appalachian Trail I maintain. Here stands of fast-growing, pioneer black locusts filled in old pastures. Japanese honeysuckle and oriental bittersweet climb the trunks and limbs of these spindly trees even more aggressively than the native Virginia creeper and grapevines. The vines smother the trees, and under the extra weight, the tree's limbs and trunks snap during the ice storms common in this region. The locusts struggle on, but instead of trees, there are inverted-V-shaped vine supports. With nothing resembling a forest canopy, the forest floor is still bathed in sunlight, encouraging more vine growth. Botanists say perhaps a fire could break the chokehold of the vines—but if even weed-tree locusts are overwhelmed, what chance do the slow growers have?

The park's few remaining pockets of virgin forest face destruction by a different imported pest. Some centuries-old hemlock groves survived in the cool, steep-sided clefts cut by streams. The rough terrain that kept out the loggers has been no protection from the woolly adelgid, which attaches itself at the base of the needles and sucks out the tree's lifeblood. Every stand in the park is infested, and they visibly weaken year by year.

The litany of biological warfare agents attacking the forest goes on and on. It's getting hard to find a dogwood without signs of infection by an anthracnose fungus, an apparently new mutant that can be deadly. Bark beetles are killing pitch and Virginia pines.

But a big question is why are these trees dying now? The woolly adelgid has been around for half a century—why are the hemlocks succumbing now, after fighting them off so long? The Shenandoah forest has been likened to a person with AIDS—vulnerable to fatal secondary infections. It can be hard to sort out blame for the deaths, hard to separate proximal and ultimate causes.

There is no substitute for large acreages to study, and the studies are finding important answers. For example, if you give those adelgids attacking the hemlocks a shot of nitrogen, their population skyrockets. Nitrogen is a plant nutrient, but like a human taking selenium, too much can be detrimental. At high levels nitrogen reduces a tree's defenses. Such findings have important policy implications because the Clean Air Act Amendments of 1990 limited sulfate but not nitrogen emissions.

Nitrates are a major ingredient of acid rain, and, downwind from the smokestacks of the Ohio and Tennessee Valleys, Shenandoah receives the heaviest load of acid deposition of any national park. (Location, the park's biggest asset, is also the biggest threat.) Rain has been measured at the pH of vinegar. For those who skipped class the day the teacher covered the pH scale, here's a less technical gauge: We bought some of those hard plastic deck chairs that discount stores sell for five bucks every spring. After a couple of years outside, their white finish comes off on your clothes if you sit in them. Rain that can leach off a plastic finish is scary stuff indeed.

Air pollution has other effects on the forest as well. Dogwood anthracnose is most virulent in trees weakened by such stresses. Acid rain leaches aluminum out of the silicates that bind it in soil. Free aluminum poisons trees that take it up in their roots or fish that ingest it from stream water.

Oaks, hickories, tulip trees, and scores of other plants display the spotted leaves of ozone damage. (Oddly enough, Shenandoah's ozone levels peak at night when it blows in from distant places.) Ozone is suspected as a major culprit in increased tree mortality rates, which studies of Appalachian forests are pegging at three to five times the historical rate.

As Tammy Wynette might have said, it's tough to be a tree these days, although every biologist I've talked with makes a point of saying that there will be some kind of forest here. "The forest of the future will be nothing like the forest of the past," one said, but nobody's making any predictions about what it will be like and none could name a tree that would actually thrive on acid rain.

Nature keeps coming back, although the replacements often seem like the second string. I can only wonder what it would be like to gather chestnuts in the fall, which residents used to sell by the hundredweight. Will the next generation wonder the same about the dogwood, a year-round treasure? Its white-flower smile declares spring has arrived; its leaves, turning deep red as early as August, color the forest for two months; once the leaves fall, red berries shine like Christmas ornaments until flocks of cedar waxwings strip them for winter sustenance.

Old-timers will declare such a forest poorer, although those who only know the new, who come here in search of a blank space on the map, can grapple with that only intellectually. If you look out from a peak, it will look like the same Great American Forest that once covered a third of the country. That is the scene from the top of Bearfence Mountain, one of the least civilization-infringed vistas in the park, bringing to mind explorer William Bartram's description that from the Blue Ridge he beheld "with rapture and astonishment, a sublimely awful scene of power and magnificence, a world of mountains piled upon mountains."

To the north and south, you see that jumbled rise and fall of the Blue Ridge itself. To the east, spur ridges reach out toward the Piedmont's foothills, rolling into the distance until curved out of sight by the Earth. To the west, you look across the valley and over the folded ridges of the Massanuttens to the Alleghenies, an Indian word meaning "endless," apt enough for the view across to the West Virginia horizon.

You actually see more forest and fewer cultivated fields than you did thirty years ago. But much of that forest lies outside the park, and at night you see the lights of many more houses. Washington is spilling out I-66; the Boston-Washington megalopolis is becoming the Portland-Richmond corridor. When plants and corporate headquarters are built in Washington's far-out suburbs, Blue Ridge hollows are within commuting distance. Subdivisions increasingly push up against the park with the appealing sales pitch that buyers can live next door to a national jewel.

Bearfence is in Greene County, one of the typical park neighbors with a love-hate relationship with growth. It's such a nice, low-cost place to live that Greene's population has grown 4 percent annually in the 1990s. Its tax base is strained by all these new school children. More industry, more jobs—more growth—would help. Natives with family land can make easy money selling off lots, much more than they can make from a hayfield or a woodlot; they can't make money off the park. Nobody wants Greene to change its rural ways, but the restrictions needed to keep it that way—telling people what they can do with their property—will become politically realistic a little after it's too late.

You can sit on Bearfence with nothing better to do than soak up sun, see what you can observe by watching, and think about what will happen to this place. As more houses and subdivisions creep toward its borders, sometimes I get a vision of the park as a single green strip, the forest a monoculture of *Ailanthus*, also known as tree of heaven, paradise tree, New York City sidewalk tree, and stinktree, a tree with the charm of a huge asparagus spike, but that nonetheless grows in air that would choke a normal tree.

But sometimes I get a different vision: that we get even more tourists on Skyline Drive, seeing the atmosphere close in on them; that we get enough of the windshield visitors out of their cars to see dying trees; that they decide it's time to do something about it.

Sitting on Bearfence, such pipe dreams seem possible. And when it's time to go, it's a quarter mile to your car. Then less than ten miles to that convenient exit from Skyline Drive. Then in two and a half hours, highway patrol willing, you can be at the Kennedy Center. Location, location, location.

Eric Seaborg is the author (with Ellen Dudley) of *American Discoveries*, winner of the Barbara Savage Award for outstanding travel writing, which tells the story of a coast-to-coast trek through wilderness, towns, and cities. The two also authored a how-to book, *Hiking and Backpacking*, writing from a perch in the Blue Ridge on the edge of Shenandoah National Park. He is a former president of the American Hiking Society and a board member of the American Discovery Trail Society. He is currently collaborating on the autobiography of his Nobel Prize–winning father Glenn Seaborg, to be published next year by Farrar, Straus, and Giroux.

ROOTS

A Mountain Retrospective:

Revisiting Southwest Virginia
Southwest Virginia

Curtis J. Badger

The waitress was tall and lanky and her brown hair had turned to gray. She placed the platter of hotcakes on the counter and gave me a look. I knew her and she knew me.

"You're the one who put George Lambie's Volkswagen in the lobby of Hillman Hall," she said with finality.

"No ma'am," I said. "As I recall, Charlie Sydnor is the one who put George's Volkswagen in the lobby of Hillman Hall."

"Oh no," she said, punching a sculpted and painted nail toward my chest. "You put the car in the dorm. Charlie Sydnor put the cow in the administration building."

Ah, the flotsam we leave in life's wake.

She had been a waitress in the snack bar at Emory & Henry College in southwest Virginia. I had been a student there and not a very good one. She remembered me for all the wrong reasons. Had I really put George's Volkswagen in the lobby of Hillman Hall? I have to admit, the possibility was real.

"That was a long time ago," I said in a tone that was more confessional than I had intended.

"Thirty years?" she asked.

"About that," I said.

"Charlie went on to become president of the college," she said.

"So I read," I said. "I wonder if anyone ever put a cow in his office?"

I remember Charlie. He was talented, bright, a student leader. He was a senior when I was a freshman. I can see him becoming president of the college. I can also see him putting a cow in the administration building and a Volkswagen in the men's dorm. Maybe I helped him. I would have done that.

* * *

I felt so grown-up then, on my own after a sheltered childhood, carrying with me the hopes of my parents, the spit-shined newness of an eighteen-year-old, eager to please, frightened of failure. The quick verdict is that it was a poor marriage, Emory & Henry and me. I wanted to write. The college wanted to teach me Old Testament and New Testament.

My affair with Emory & Henry was a teenage marriage, full of passion but little resolve. Four years, no degree, but many wonderful memories. I could have done better. I could have made those 8 A.M. classes, could have put forth more effort, could have acted as if I gave a damn. Emory could have taught me how to write, how to channel that part of me spinning out of control into the written word.

It is interesting now to go back, insulated by the passage of thirty years, with wife and son, to see Hillman Hall, wondering how I got that Volkswagen up the steps and through the doors and into the lobby. In my time the college seemed isolated, an island of Protestantism in the mountains of rural southwest Virginia. It could have been anywhere, a self-contained community centered around the tenets of Methodism, adrift from the larger community of the mountains, of rural Virginia, where coal mining and tobacco farming, and the grinding essence of poverty, seemed pervasive.

But today I find that the college is no longer apart from the community, but a part of it. Appalachian studies are central to the curriculum. There are courses in creative writing, and the college holds an annual writers' conference and publishes an anthology of writing, mainly from regional authors. Perhaps I met Emory & Henry too early in life. Perhaps now our relationship would be more ful-filling.

Going back to southwest Virginia recently, I realized what I had missed, not only from my immature approach to academics, but from my ambivalence to the larger community of Emory and especially from the natural communities of places like the Clinch and Holston Rivers, Whitetop, Mount Rogers, the trout streams, lakes, ridges, and valleys of the Appalachians.

When I first went to Emory, the landscape seemed foreign. I had grown up on the Virginia coast, exploring the remote islands and salt marshes of my home, comfortable there. I realize now how much these two places have in common, how different they are at first glance, yet how alike. Both the Eastern Shore and southwest Virginia are on the periphery of the Commonwealth, in ways that are both literal and symbolic. In both places there is a suspicion of having been left out. The Eastern Shore is separated from the rest of the state by water; sometimes, on maps, the little peninsula is omitted altogether. Re-garding the southwest, there is the perception in some parts that the state's western boundary is Roanoke.

The remoteness of both the Eastern Shore and southwest Virginia has created a certain kinship. There is poverty and few good jobs, so both areas are offered the economic development schemes no one else wants: prisons, soil remediation, medical waste treatment plants, and the like. But both areas possess numbing beauty; salt meadow vistas and wilderness ocean beaches in the east, rolling mountains and mu-sical trout streams in the west.

The people, too, are alike—friendly but reticent, generous, living lives tied to the land, harvesting seafood from the bays, grain from a fertile hillside. Both are people of faith, in the southwest, belief in the miracle of germination, the splitting of seed, photosynthesis, growth, harvest. In the east, faith in the predictability of tides, the conviction that the flood tide will rise only so far, and then ebb.

There also is fierce pride of place. I feel it regarding my home on Virginia's Eastern Shore. I resent those who, to turn a quick buck, would do things to diminish its natural richness. My wife Lynn and I were hiking the Virginia Creeper Trail near Damascus not long ago and we remarked at how clean the trail was, when around the next bend came a troop of Boy Scouts on a litter pickup mission. They

Indiana bat

had only a few gum wrappers to show for their work, but their determination was commendable.

Both southwest Virginia and the Eastern Shore are discovering that their natural assets can be used wisely to improve the quality of life of the community without endangering the resource itself. The Virginia Coast Reserve represents the last of the coastal wilderness in the East, a stretch of unspoiled sandy beach that extends some sixty miles from Cape Charles northward. The Nature Conservancy owns forty-five thousand acres here on fourteen barrier islands. Rather than erecting a fence around this natural area and ordering people out, the Conservancy recognized that humans are a component of the natural system and has worked with local people to create ways to use the resource without devaluing it. Projects include clams raised in an aquaculture setting, nature-based tourism, marketing of specialty food crops, and even residential housing.

The Conservancy has also been active in southwest Virginia, with the Virginia Chapter having established a field office in Abingdon several years ago. As in the east, the focus is on water; not the estuarine system of bays and marshes, but swift running rivers and streams that support one of the most diverse ecosystems on the planet.

The Clinch Valley is a swath of high country stretching through eight of Virginia's westernmost counties and into Tennessee. It encompasses the watersheds of the Clinch, Powell, and Holston Rivers, and includes Mount Rogers, the highest point in the state. Within its boundaries are literally hundreds of rare species, making the region invaluable to biologists and underlining the necessity of protecting the streams, rivers, and rivulets that determine the quality of the water and thus the quality of life.

The Conservancy owns six preserves in southwest Virginia and has been working with local governments, landowners, and citizen groups to protect other fragile ecosystems while using the resource to improve the quality of life of the region. Residents of southwest Virginia are finding that the rich history and natural beauty of the area attract people who will spend money, yet treat the area gently and with respect.

In my days at Emory, Abingdon was a tired old tobacco and coal town, its Main Street lined with sagging hotels, apartments, and stores. Today there are galleries, restaurants, offices, and antiques shops. Out on Interstate 81 are hotel and restaurant chains, strip malls, and fast-food shops. Not pretty in everyone's eye, but evidence that better times have come.

Abingdon has seen its sprawl in recent years, but it takes only a short drive to get to the core of what makes southwest Virginia special. On a recent spring morning we joined the Conservancy's Don Gowan for a visit to Pinnacle Natural Area Preserve, which lies at the junction of Clinch River and Big Cedar Creek, about a half hour north of Abingdon.

We hiked across a pasture and into a forest, where a trail led to a rocky outcrop towering six hundred feet over the Clinch and Big Cedar. Awesome is an overused word, but I can think of none that describes this landscape better. The Conservancy was instrumental in creating this preserve, working with the previous owner, Russell County, and the Virginia Department of Conservation and Recreation.

The natural beauty of the area is emphatic. The river cuts like a silver blade through the green hillsides, disappearing into folds of mountains, which in turn disappear into a veil of haze. Once off the path, there is no evidence of the human hand as far as we can see—no roads, no houses, no hotels and restaurants. And there is comfort in knowing that people are working to make it forever so.

While first-time visitors are struck by the physical beauty of the place, there is more to it than meets the eye. The calcium carbonate rocks on which we stood have been weathering for more than 400 million years. The dissolving action of water on limestone and dolomite has created some unusual rock formations, not the least of which is the outcropping for which the Pinnacle Preserve is named. The weathering of the rock has produced calcium-rich soils that support wildflowers and ferns, as well as impressive stands of white cedar, which give Big Cedar Creek its name. And the limestone bedrock that underlies the region is honeycombed with hundreds of caves that are home to at least fifty globally rare cave organisms.

But the key to the health of this preserve—and of the surrounding eco-region—is water, in this case the Clinch River and Big Cedar. The Virginia sections of the Clinch and Powell Rivers are the only undammed, unspoiled headwaters of the Tennessee River system, and they support the most ecologically diverse region of the state, with more than four hundred rare plants and animals. Because of the abundant calcium, the waters of the Clinch support a wide population of mussels, some of which are found nowhere else. Calcium, that building block of better bones, is crucial to the formation of shell, and the quality of water is vital to filter-feeding animals such as mussels.

The Conservancy, Don said, is assisting local landowners in reducing silt and bacterial contamination. In one program, the Conservancy is working with cattle growers to provide drinking stations for the cattle instead of having the animals wade in rivers and streams. In another, the Conservancy is working with coal companies to reduce acid drainage and chemical contamination from abandoned mines.

There still are threats, and there still are scars from old injuries. But in walking these hills, driving the back roads, and in talking with local residents, one cannot help but feel optimistic. There seems to be a pride of place, a commitment to protect this natural heritage.

* * *

South of Abingdon, Route 58 winds through pastureland and farms, crosses the Middle Fork of the Holston River, and enters Damascus, an industry town built around the promise of iron ore. In 1886, J. D. Imboden, a speculator in mining and the steel industry, incorporated a small farming community called Mock's Mill and renamed it Damascus, hoping the town would replicate the success of its namesake in Syria, which had once been the steel capital of the Mediterranean.

Damascus never became a steel capital, but investors laid the groundwork for a railroad linking Damascus with Abingdon and the great wide world of Norfolk & Western Railroad. While iron ore didn't pan out, timber did. The railroad opened in 1900, and in the next two decades logging went on at a fever pitch in the Whitetop area, with narrow-gauge tracks snaking into the coves and hollows of the mountains, extracting the valuable virgin timber.

The Virginia-Carolina Railway hauled millions of tons of lumber, iron ore, passengers, and supplies until gradually the supply of timber ran out. The railroad no longer was profitable; the lumber companies left town. Norfolk & Western, which had acquired the railroad in 1919, continued to provide service on a reduced basis, until finally it eliminated passenger service in 1962, and made its last freight run in 1977. The little railroad, nicknamed the Virginia Creeper, had become part of the colorful history of southwest Virginia.

Meanwhile, the clearcut hillsides of Whitetop had been sold by the timber companies to the federal government for inclusion in the national forest system. By the time the Virginia Creeper made its last run, the forest had regenerated, with nice stands of yellow poplars, hemlocks, maples, oaks, and hickory trees. When Norfolk & Western closed the line, it sold the track as scrap metal, and the right-of-way through the Jefferson National Forest was purchased by the U.S. Forest Service. The towns of Abingdon and Damascus bought the remainder. In 1986 Congress designated the 34.3 miles of right-of-way as a National Recreation Trail, and the Virginia Creeper was back in business. Although the old steam engine remains parked at the trailhead in Abingdon, more than twenty-five thousand people travel along the roadbed each year—by foot, by bike, and by horse.

The railroad has over the years reflected the fortunes of Damascus. When service dwindled, the town was virtually cut off, its economic tie severed. But today, the popularity of the rail-trail has revitalized Damascus. On a recent visit, we noted several new businesses; a new and wider bridge was being constructed downtown over Laurel Creek. There were numerous out-of-state cars, many of which sported bike racks.

Damascus had been a popular stopover among hikers on the Appalachian Trail (AT) for years, but the opening of the Creeper Trail, which coincides with the AT near town, brought in a wider, and perhaps more affluent, clientele. The nature-based tourism industry sparked by the Creeper Trail has not had the sudden economic and social impact logging had between 1900 and 1920, but it certainly will benefit the community for much longer than twenty years.

Phoebe Cartwright retreated to Damascus from the business world and in 1992 began operating Blue Blaze Bike and Shuttle Service out of her home. She has since moved her business into a former garage and, because of a growing clientele, has added a staff of van drivers and bike mechanics. For a modest fee, Phoebe will load your bike onto her trailer and drive you to the trailhead at Whitetop Station, where you can ride, or, more accurately, coast, eighteen miles down a gentle grade back to Damascus. If you have no bike, she will rent you one, and if you opt to ride the full 34.3 miles to Abingdon, she will arrange to have you picked up there.

We opted for the latter, deciding that we wanted to experience the trail in its entirety. We had earlier walked a portion of it, near what had been the Watauga Station, about four miles outside Abingdon. At that time we were looking for birds, so we ambled along at an easy pace, binoculars ready. It had been a memorable hike, too, in that within a span of about five minutes we saw both yellow-billed and black-billed cuckoos.

We didn't bring the binoculars on the bike ride, just a compact camera, peanut butter and banana sandwiches, and water bottles filled with lemonade. Phoebe dropped us off and we began the gentle descent to Damascus. The trail crosses brooks, streams, and hollows, with more than one hundred wooden trestles in the 34.3 miles. These became the highlight of the ride; nearly all afford great views, sometimes of a swift trout stream, sometimes a lush valley, and, near mile 8, the confluence of the Middle and South Forks of the Holston River.

The portion of the trail from Whitetop Station to Damascus is the wildest, crisscrossing the Appalachian Trail, running parallel to Whitetop Laurel Creek for much of the way. It is a spectacular place to ride, although with the trail descending, the temptation is to speed through it. Most of this section is in the Jefferson National Forest, while the Damascus-to-Abingdon portion crosses private land. The trail becomes noticeably flatter as it nears Damascus, and between Damascus and Abingdon there is very little grade.

I'm glad we rode the entire trail, but on the next trip, I think I'll stick to the eastern section, perhaps beginning in Damascus and heading uphill. That way, I'll slow down, stop now and then, and fully enjoy this opportunity to experience a wild part of southwest Virginia.

* * *

It is a nine-hour ride from Abingdon to our home on the Eastern Shore, and although we were anxious to get into the rhythm of the interstate, we made one last exit at Meadowview and drove down to Emory, through the gates of the college, down the hill behind Wiley Hall, and parked in front of the snack bar and Hillman Hall, the men's dorm.

It was early summer and no one was around. The snack bar was closed, and only a few maintenance workers were in Hillman. I walked in through the side door and climbed the stairs to the second floor. Room 211 was on the right, a short distance down the hall. The door was unlocked, and so I entered. The built-in bunk beds and desks were as I remembered them. I had the top bunk and the desk on the left side of the room. In winter, I kept cartons of milk on the window ledge. My roommate and I had bought a red carpet; we played Kingston Trio records.

On the first floor the lobby is in the center of the building, with hallways on either side, and the housemother's apartment is in the rear, just beyond the reception desk. Did she see us push and lift George's old blue Beetle up the stairway and through the doors? Did she peek out from her doorway and stifle a laugh? Did she sit down for coffee with the snack bar waitress the next morning and go into great detail about those crazy boys?

I honestly don't know. She is gone now, and Hillman Hall is facing an extensive renovation, with the entryway, and presumably the lobby, to be rebuilt. I have some advice for them. Make that stairway a little less steep, and make those doors nice and wide.

Curtis J. Badger lives with his family on Onancock Creek on Virginia's Eastern Shore. He is the author of thirty books on natural history, wildlife art, and Eastern Shore history. His most recent book is *Bellevue Farm: Exploring Virginia's Coastal Countryside*, a collection of "personal natural history essays" based upon four years of exploring a seaside farm owned by The Nature Conservancy.

The Nature Conservancy began working in the Clinch Valley, one of the most ecologically significant areas in the United States, in 1984, and now owns six nature preserves in the region.

ONLY IN THE LAND OF GOSHEN
Goshen Pass

Katie Letcher Lyle

Goshen Pass has been my favorite playground most of my life. What I have lately discovered is that, for such an apparently supernal, wild area, fragility may be its most salient feature.

For sheer awe, there's Natural Bridge adorning the county named for it. For libraries, learning, and boutiques, Lexington is the place. But for the jewel of Rockbridge County, wind your way north and west fifteen miles out Route 39 to Goshen Pass. There, the north fork of the James winds and gushes between dramatic limestone cliffs through a boulder-choked five-mile gorge to enter the Valley of Virginia, meandering past Lexington, Buena Vista, and Glasgow, and on to the Chesapeake Bay.

My mother and a friend with a kid my age first took me there in our homemade bathing suits in 1943, where Mama perched on a rock. Her habit of enduring weekly tortures at the beauty parlor left her scalp angrily red, and as long as I knew her, she never went swimming. She wasn't going to ruin her set.

It was early summer and overcast, the water pellucid green, white where it foamed in the rapids. Boulders as big as houses loomed above us, jutting out of the cliffs overhead. Evergreens and sycamores rustled in the constant breeze. We'd just driven east from San Diego to come live with Daddy's parents in Lexington while he fought Japanese in the Pacific.

I remember how big the pass seemed, how swift the water, when the woman who wasn't my mother persuaded me to jump off the rock I stood on at the lower end of Indian Pool, and into her arms. From then on, I preferred river to beach.

After Daddy returned from the war, we spent two more years in the Marine Corps, in Norfolk, then California, before returning for good to Virginia.

I begged to get driven to Goshen every day in summer, year after year. My three siblings and I, and often assorted friends, would hang our heads out the windows in the hot car until we came under the dark rocks and trees of the pass, instantly ten degrees cooler. We'd shiver, even on the hottest days, getting wet bit by bit, screaming or stolid (I was a screamer), until, finally immersed, we'd slide down rapids, ripping the seats of our bathing suits, splash each other, jump recklessly off rocks, even swim a bit. Daddy would strip down to nothing or, if Mama or others were along, a disreputable pair of droopy woollen shorts with a drawstring, don his diving mask, then crash in without flinching, maneuvering on his stomach around boulders to case the pools for fish he could come back and catch another day.

Mama had a friend who loved picnicking at a particularly dramatic overhang called Devil's Kitchen, who always brought *deviled* eggs and *devil's food* cake. It amused her, and suited us fine. We'd spread a blanket on a nearly level rock in the river, eat ourselves silly, and lie in the sun with baby-oil-iodine slathered on, waiting for an hour to pass so we could slip back into the water.

When we got older, we'd wash our hair in the river, convinced that Goshen water made it shinier. We'd never heard of pollution. We sang a song a friend wrote, plunking along on our ukeleles, that started: *I got a notion for Goshen, the best place around to go; to Hell with the ocean . . . .* On summer nights in high school the ultimate dare was to strip and skinny-dip in Blue Hole.

We went in winter when it was always windy, and rawer than in town, dirty snow lingering for months in deep hollows where sun never pierced. The water was milky gray-green, and icicles hung as thick as stalactites. On the mountains, ice split the rocks. Once a boulder bigger than our car lay smack in the middle of the road, and we had to turn back.

pink trillium

We'd hike up Laurel Run in early spring when the water was light green and ice-cold to see the speckle-leafed yellow dogtooth violets, to spot the first pink trillium, the diminutive blue-purple wild iris. Occasionally cadets or Washington and Lee students would get killed trying to canoe or tube the swollen water of late spring that hid the boulders, when pea-soup silt made the rapids invisible until it was too late. One year, a cadet on a scholarship in honor of a boy who'd drowned years before, drowned.

As the sun returned northward, and we could see summer vacation on the horizon, we knew to watch for snakes and poison ivy, as the water softened to its summer color, clear gold-green, and the landscape thickened from the tender greens of spring to the solid dense emerald of July.

A blond boy, somewhere between heed and hedonism, would dive
into water that was too shallow, to show off—while I waited para-
lyzed with fear—and come up spouting, grinning at my terror. He'd
pretend remorse, and clamber up the rock to where we all lay on
towels burning and gossiping, enfold me in his arms, crooning fake
apologies while the chorus of girls shrieked. I'd struggle to get my
hands between my hot skin and his dripping cold arms, my flesh
recoiling from his wet flesh. We'd slip into the bottle green water, to
howls from the upper gallery. I'd look up at their tanned laughing
faces honeycombed from the sun glancing off the lapping water, off
guard long enough for him to duck me. Sometimes we would kiss in
the water, and I felt embarrassed, for the river was clear from their
vantage, but honored, too, even beautiful.

Goshen Pass, I came to know, was almost a sacred site to generations of Virginia Military Institute (VMI) cadets and Washington
and Lee boys, and the girls they imported from nearby colleges each
spring to sun and drink beer and woo. Every spring of my college
days at Hollins, engagement diamonds sprouted like daffodils. "I got
it last weekend, at Goshen," a besotted classmate would chirp, wig-
gling her ring around to make it flash.

Part of the mystique of Goshen Pass was the stories. The biggest
rattlesnakes in the East lurked in Goshen Pass: in the 1880s, there'd
been one more than eight feet long and big as a man's thigh, killed at
Devil's Kitchen by someone my grandfather knew.

The river running through Goshen Pass is named for Matthew
Fontaine Maury, head of the Confederate Navy, "Pathfinder of the
Seas," professor of meteorology at VMI, whose body lay unburied
for seven months because he requested that it be carried through the
pass en route to his final resting place *when the rhododendron bloomed.*
Though Maury died in February 1873, at most four months before
the blooming, his request was inexplicably neglected until September,
when the coffin was decked with autumn leaves—too little too late,
some might say.

The mountains rising above Goshen on both sides are pocked with limestone caves, and at least one painted cave wall has been discovered. The remains of fires in that cave have been carbon-dated to as far back as A.D. 875. Mysteriously, there are in the area an abundance of Archaic (8000–1000 B.C.) sites of occupation, but a dearth for the Woodland period (1000 B.C.–European contact). Near the eastern end of the pass was a large mound, about which George Washington Bagby wrote in 1872, "we rummaged an Indian mound, a very mass of bones. . . ." In 1901 Edward P. Valentine excavated that mound for his Richmond museum. Today the Valentine Museum claims that the "eighty perfect skulls, a number of nearly perfect skeletons, and the . . . bones of more than four hundred people and eight dogs," which were "shipped to the Museum for scientific study" are, inexplicably, lost. Nobody knows what tribes or groups they belonged to. Nobody measured the bones. Nobody catalogued the grave goods.

Sometime back, the rash of reported UFO sightings all over America included one from Goshen Pass. Someone called the sheriff: supposedly three cars, two going one way, one the other, were stopped late one night by a strange craft blocking the road. All three drivers got out, noted each other as well as the craft, but strangely, never spoke to each other. Just got back in their cars and drove on after the craft rose slowly from the road, then vanished.

Rockbridge Countians share their love for this natural area with each new generation. My children know what my grandfather and father taught me: there used to be wolves and panthers in Goshen Pass. My grandfather, when a boy, tamed a fox cub found motherless in the field by Wilson Springs, and kept it awhile. *Halfway between a cat and a dog,* is what he told me. Bison once grazed that same field. We've heard a bobcat scream, an absolutely horrifying wail. We know the plaintive call of the whippoorwill.

My husband the bird watcher has taught us to recognize phoebes, Louisiana waterthrushes, pileated woodpeckers, scarlet tanagers, green herons, and kingfishers. Ravens, kestrels, and vultures ply the skies over the pass; bald eagles and ospreys pass through. On summer nights we hear the eerie cries of screech owls. We all know arbor vitae, scores of different ferns, oaks, cedars and pines, hemlock, mountain laurel and rhododendron. We gather morels, watercress, chanterelles, wineberries, catnip.

Once, my husband and children and I saw a huge shambly black dog lope across the road in front of the car. Only as it disappeared into underbrush and boulders did we realize we'd seen a black bear— hadn't we? Each year, hunters with fierce dogs and walkie-talkies tree and shoot the shy bears for the sport of it. Rarely do they eat the meat.

* * *

Goshen Pass, at least as long as white men have lived hereabouts, has been under siege.

Rivers and passes are the natural highways through virgin territory. The settlers could brook no affront to westward expansion. The first attempted road through the pass, really only a path, begun shortly after 1800, crossed and recrossed the river at shallows, usually rapids, and wove narrowly under the steep cliffs. High water periodically washed out the roadway, gouged gulleys with freshets, and eroded the banks with wet-weather springs.

In the 1850s, the railroad stop leading westward was at the far end of the pass. To Lexingtonians and other travelers who needed to traverse it to catch westbound trains, Goshen Pass became a bête noire, "a most execrable turnpike," and "a succession of dismal traps and pitfalls for the unwary traveler." The road through Goshen, a local complained, "surpasses the plank road in the energy and abruptness of its concussions." "A gigantic and horrible chasm," concluded one survivor.

The nineteenth century raised hydrotherapy from fad to science, and Goshen Pass has in its environs just about every kind of spring. A mile below the pass is Rockbridge Baths, a lithium spring, known then, as now, for a calming effect on the brain. Right at the eastern entrance is a tiny island in the river with two springs on it: a small iron spring, whose waters seep reddish brown and smell like blood; and a vigorous sulphur spring, with benefits galore internal and external, its waters still smelling just like Clearasil, that sulphur-based mud we used to dab on pimples. Just above the pass is a spring of "sweet chalybeate"—an iron salt believed to be a tonic for anemia, nervous diseases, weakness, and "female complaints." And several miles south is the once-fashionable Rockbridge Alum Springs where folks went to get rid of diarrhea and scrofula. All the waters hereabouts test positive for calcium, or lime, compounds. In the 1800s, the springs vied for the most effectiveness and the most cures, collecting testimonials from satisfied customers. The springs thrived, drawing summer visitors to and through Goshen Pass on horseback, in wagons, from the hotter eastern part of Virginia. Some came as far as Lexington on the C&O Canal.

During the Civil War the pass was four times guarded by VMI cadets, summoned when it was believed that General Averill would attempt to march his northern troops through the gorge. The cadets bivouacked at the eastern end, in the cabins and mile-long field at Wilson Springs. Averill did eventually occupy Lexington in June of 1864, but he arrived by another route.

In 1870 a flood devastated Goshen Pass, and indeed the entire river, washing away even the coffin, shipped by packet boat from Richmond upstream to Lexington, for General Robert E. Lee. Afterwards, a passable road was cut and blasted on the south side of the river for the entirety of Goshen Pass. The plan was to lay a train track, but that eventually proved impossible.

In 1928 the Virginia Public Service Company applied to construct a dam at the upper end of the pass for a power plant, to meet the growing needs of the state. The fight against what would obviously have ruined the pass forever, leaving the streambed dry most of the time, was led by Washington and Lee professor W. D. Hoyt, who was soon joined by the fierce ranks of the Garden Club of Virginia. Major A. Willis Robertson of Lexington, chairman of the State Commission of Game and Inland Fisheries (and father of evangelist Pat Robertson), who lobbied trenchantly for the dam, turned out to have been retained as counsel for the Virginia Public Service Company to the tune of $4000 a year, a princely sum at the time. The discovery of this conflict of interests prompted his resignation as counsel, but soured public opinion against the project, which had begun to look sleazy. Robertson's defense was that his special interest was the preservation of fishing rights, and that impounded waters offer the best fishing!

In the year 1929 such gentle organizations as the Daughters of the American Revolution, the Association for the Preservation of Virginia Antiquities, and the Young Women's Christian Association dubbed themselves "The Committee for the Preservation of Goshen Pass." They mobbed the Virginia legislature, wrote letters, and urged landowners to hold out against the power company. Throughout the state, editorials condemned the scheme.

In the end, the stock market crash drained the financial strength of both sides, and Goshen Pass was let alone yet a while longer.

In 1938, the state decided the road through Goshen Pass needed modernizing. This again roused the citizenry to protest. Chastened by the power plant episode, the state, "with due regard to the fears of the Ladies Garden clubs," improved the road sensitively, landscaping the shoulders and building stone retaining walls.

World War II came and went, and in the postwar period, other priorities arose. The road through Goshen Pass was heralded as a model highway, as travelers and locals continued to enjoy this magical place.

After driving through the snowy pass in January of 1954, a vigilant outdoorsman raised the alarm that severe timber cutting was occurring on the north side of the river at the western end of the pass, visible and ugly through the winter-bare trees.

Once more Rockbridge citizens roused themselves, and three local people put up the money to purchase the miscreant's timber rights.

Financial support came once again from many local residents and the
Virginia Garden Club. As the result of an editorial in a Charlottesville
paper, an eleemosynary group called the Perry Foundation offered
about three-quarters of the total needed to turn the tract forever into
a protected area. The Virginia Park Service accepted the land, and the
north side of the river was supposedly permanently protected. Five
years later, another Lexingtonian successfully engineered the sale to
the state of nearly sixteen thousand acres on the south bank. This
time, the Federal Wildlife Service provided the majority of the money,
and the Goshen Wildlife Management Area maintains the acreage
today. It appeared the pass would be safe forever.

But the Virginia Public Service Company still owned the land designated for the 1929 power plant. Through a complicated series of
trades and sales, that land finally sold in 1962 to the National Capital Area Council of the Boy Scouts of America, for a camp to serve
Washington, D.C., area Scouts.

Needing deep water for boating and swimming, the Boy Scouts
quietly dammed one of the two major tributaries that make up the
Maury, promising to let water out of their lake in time of drought.
Though they have done so, concern arose early about water quality.
The water released is silty; flowing into the pass, it settles on the
bottom to smother the food sources of the fish. Above the pass are
other potentially toxic industries, safe only until high water comes
and washes their poisons into the stream.

There have been several unexplained fish kills in recent years, a
snail kill that stripped the rocks of small black indigenous snails, odd
pockets of foam and algae where none had been before. The willow
grass has disappeared. Though the bass, carp, and sun-perch have returned, the snails never have. And no one really knows how safe the
Boy Scout dam is, and what would happen if a wall of water should
come ripping down the pass.

In 1972, the state of Virginia unveiled a plan to "develop" Goshen
Pass, to allow no stopping along the road, to build riding trails and a

"whitewater walk" for those who cared to park, then hike miles to their favorite spots. The formidable Hydra of the local citizenry rose up again, appalled at "campsites," multi-acred parking lots, and the removal of all the beloved roadside pulloffs where we park to swim and picnic. The Rockbridge County Board of Supervisors expressed their opinion of the scheme by unanimously rejecting plans for a "small sewage treatment plant" *upstream* of the pass, to serve the proposed "Visitors' Center."

In the past, a century or more has elapsed between major floods, giving the river a chance to recover, establish new vegetation. But with more woods cleared for pastureland, paved roads, parking lots, commercial land overtaking wilderness, hard rains bring heavy runoffs. When floods come, as they have recently, every few years instead of once a century, the river never gets a chance to revive. Whether from man's depredations or changing weather patterns, these constant floods have changed the pass forever, cutting deep into the outsides of curves, washing out trees and other vegetation that prevent the banks from eroding, depositing boulders, pebbles, and mud in new places, widening and shallowing the river below the pass.

Goshen Pass, still one of the loveliest places on earth, remains, despite all the best efforts of so many people, immensely fragile. Its future cannot be certain until all the private land is free from the threat of development. Even then, somebody in the capitol can undoubtedly dream up another travesty. The water quality is anxiously monitored today by groups of environmentalists.

Its name, Goshen, is from the Bible, of course, which tells us, "And the hail smote throughout all the land . . . all that was in the field, both man and beast; and the hail smote every herb of the field and brake every tree of the field. Only in the land of Goshen . . . was there no hail" (Exodus 9:25-26). I used to think that was, metaphorically speaking, true. Nothing could or would hurt Goshen Pass. My grandfather, Greenlee Letcher, fought the 1929 dam and power plant. My father, General John Letcher, was the outdoorsman who spotted the denuded tract in January 1954, and put up a third of the money to buy the timber rights. My husband, Royster Lyle, was a leader of the outraged activists of 1972. I know firsthand the battles these men have fought. Goshen Pass's history may be a cautionary tale for all who care about their own wild places of the world.

Acknowledgments: The author wishes to thank the following people for pointing me to articles, lending personal papers, and/or allowing me interviews: M.W. Paxton, Jr., Julia (Coates) Littlefield, George Tolley, Keith Egloff, Deborah Woodward, Doug Harwood, Jay Gilliam, David Harbor, Sam Crickenberger, Paul Bugas, and the recently deceased Colonel John Reeves.

Katie Letcher Lyle is the author of sixteen books—poetry, novels, historical nonfiction, and nature—including *When the Fighting Is All Over*, a memoir of growing up and making peace with her Marine Corps general father. A writer, teacher, folksinger, and speaker, her short fiction has been published in *Viva, Shenandoah,* and the *Virginia Quarterly Review*.

WILD IN THE CITY: THE URBAN JAMES RIVER
James River

Elizabeth Seydel Morgan

The James River literally falls into the city of Richmond. After gathering the waters of the Alleghenies, of the Valley of Virginia and the Blue Ridge, the James bends and curves through the Piedmont, then plunges through the western city limits into 7 miles of rapids that will drop it 105 feet into calm tidal water just past the high rises of downtown Richmond.

It is pretty amazing to live within walking distance of such whitewater, but for years I hardly knew the river was there. When I left my parents' home in Atlanta to move to Richmond, I was twenty-one. In Atlanta, too, I had lived near a river, though the Chattahoochee didn't so obviously surge through downtown. Still, it was a large and beautiful and polluted river that the people in my youth completely ignored. In my childhood and high-school years I knew no one who canoed it, swam in it, fished it, or explored it. Only occasionally would we cross over it, teenagers on our way to party at Robinson's Tropical Gardens.

In the sixties, in Richmond, the James River for me might as well have been the Chattahoochee. I saw it when I used its bridges to get to the southside—which was rare because I lived and worked and shopped and went to my OBs and pediatricians all on the northside. But in Richmond, unlike Atlanta, I did know someone who had used the river when he was young. My good friend Bill told me of his long solitary confinement in the hospital with typhoid when even his mother was not allowed in his quarantine room. He had contracted typhoid fever in the fifties, the probable result of fishing or swimming in the James below Twenty-second Street, where the city's raw sewerage was discharged into its river. Astonishing as it is, we did not stop using our river as a sewer until 1958, when primary treatment of wastewater began. It was not until 1973 that the secondary system was installed.

I can remember the large, bold signs that discouraged use of the James at the few places where it was accessible at all. No Swimming. No Boating. Thinking back, I decided the river must have been polluted during the years I was raising young children. But Ralph R. White, the leading expert on the urban James, the naturalist for the James River Park System, which opened in 1971–1972, tells me that this was not the case. He says the James River "is one of the great examples of the success of the Clean Water Act of 1969" and by 1970 it was not polluted. The area along Riverside Drive where I remember the signs, in fact, was never polluted. White says the city warned people away, afraid of the ramifications of dangerous rapids and public use in general.

So between Bill's typhoid and the signs on the riverside—combined with the difficulty of parking—I had little inclination to take my toddlers for a dip or a walk or a birdwatch along their city river.

I only know in hindsight from the end of the century how all of this changed. I know it changed for me personally because of the many happy memories I have of the river in the late seventies, eighties, nineties, and just a few days ago. Memories involving dipping and walking and parking and also rafting, canoeing, meditating, sketching, tubing, picnicking, swimming, exploring and learning. I am aware now of the hundreds of dedicated people and scores of organizations—like Ralph White, R. B. Young, and the Falls of the James Committee—who worked to restore the river. They gave this present to my family and me and changed my perception from indifference to love of the great natural resource in my city.

My earliest river memory involves simply sitting beside the James where the whitewater begins—possibly trespassing—and looking at it. At some point in the early seventies the riverside became a refuge for me. I wanted to be a poet, but as a high-school teacher and mother of three young children, I had no real privacy, no space. A patch of ground downriver from the Huguenot Bridge became my "room of one's own." I'd long known that sitting in a folding chair in front of the Atlantic Ocean was the best place to be alone in a crowd. The sight and pounding rhythm of breaking waves draws your attention from any distraction and allows your mind to flow. But I had to discover the similar effect of rushing water breaking over rock, the different but also meditative sound of current.

My most recent river experience is also one of looking. I was seeing the urban James through the eyes of my seven-year-old granddaughter. Cameron's second-grade teacher had given the students an assignment to take pictures and make an album of the sights of their hometown: Jefferson's Capitol, skyscrapers, islands in the James, bridges, and the whitewater rapids running under them. We drove downtown on a sparkling, cloudless day in late fall, parked beside the river near the emptied canal which is being restored as a canal walk, and walked across the footbridge that now spans the river to Belle Isle. She skipped ahead on the undulating roadway of this beautifully designed bridge. (I myself felt a little nervous suspended over rapids. I wanted her to hold my hand.) In the middle we stopped for the photo ops: with her little disposable Kodak, Cameron got pictures of the city skyline rising from the river, its tall buildings clustered near the place where Christopher Newport and Captain John Smith ("yes, the *Pocahontas* John Smith") had been forced to stop. Their party had first sailed a shallop upstream in May of 1607, confronted the impassable rapids at the fall line and returned to Jamestown, but not before planting a cross and naming the river, also, for their king. Cameron pointed her camera ahead at Belle

Isle, a fifty-four acre island in the heart of Richmond that is now part of the James River Park System. She took a picture of the remains of the old bridge, which Hurricane Camille had destroyed in 1969. We walked along the island's paths, reading information about its history as Indian fishing village, notorious Confederate prisoner-of-war camp, and site of a "historic iron and steel mill." When I told her that her grandfather had once worked for Old Dominion Iron and Steel Corporation, she took a picture of its remaining sheds. Belle Isle became a part of her history too.

Walking back over the footbridge, Cameron leaned over the side of the railing to take pictures of rocks and rapids, then turned for one picture of an apprehensive grandmother.

* * *

I suppose I was a little apprehensive when I took my first whitewater rafting trip more than twenty years ago. I'd been invited to join five other moms-of-young-children to give this new adventure in Richmond a try. But in my memory I wasn't scared a bit as our six-person guided raft approached the Class IV rapids of the lower section. For one thing, I didn't know what a Class IV rapid was, nor did I know back then of the famous dangers of Hollywood Rapids or Pipeline. (Today my grown son, Matt, an experienced kayaker and canoeist who spent a lot of his teenage years on the James, tells me that Hollywood and Pipeline are equal in difficulty to any rapid he's ever paddled. In his canoeing guide, *Virginia White Water,* Roger Corbett directs readers through Hollywood Rapid with challenging words: "This big, complex, deadly rapid is entered on the right, close to the island [Belle Isle].") Well, these directions would have been more chilling than challenging to someone who had never been on white water, but our expert rafting guide—though giving us plenty of good advice about paddling hard when she yelled "kick it," and about what to do if you fell overboard—did not if my memory serves ever use the word "deadly."

I remember my heart was pounding as we approached Hollywood Cemetery on the high bluff to our left and heard the rapids below. And I remember screaming with delight as we plunged over the big drop between boulders and got thoroughly drenched. But I don't remember screaming out of fear for my life.

river otters

The trip our raft took, still available today from the Richmond Raft Company, is also the route of intermediate-expert canoeists and kayakers. You start out from the Pony Pasture (the park at the head of the falls) into current which Corbett's guide calls "Class I rock garden type rapids with a few Class II chutes interspersed"; paddle downstream in flatwater to minor, then medium and major rapids; take out from the calm, tidal waters below the Fall Line. Though none of our group was "woman overboard" on this trip, the water was washing over us often. It was my introduction to the exhilaration of being *on* a wild river, after first experiencing the serenity of sitting at its side.

Women introduced me to the James, and two in particular taught me just about everything I know about its pleasures. Amanda Macaulay and Temple Martin both taught girls as well as boys to become "Watermen" in courses at St. Catherine's and St. Christopher's Schools, where I taught English. "Watermen" was the outdoor skills course;

"James River" was an intensive study of the entire river both historically and ecologically. Both of my friends went on to initiate and direct other programs on the river as well. This is what they did professionally; they took their landlubbing friend down to the James for fun.

Amanda and I went from playing around among the rocks with our children, to floating lazily in inner tubes on outings to get away from our children, to the next step of her teaching me to paddle a canoe. I'd been in a canoe a few times on a lake, once on a calm river, and of course I had helped paddle that raft through all the falls of the urban James. Amanda had to show me that none of these experiences had taught me how to control a canoe among rocks. She showed me how to lash and unlash a canoe to a station wagon, portage it (though she did most of the hoisting), and put in upstream from the rapids. There she directed me to the bow and taught me the cross-bow draw stroke and the pry stroke. The person in the bow needs these strokes to avoid the obstacles, she said, "since you'll be the first to see the rocks coming at us."

Our first excursion took us through a little chute of water where I indeed saw the rocks coming at us—they looked like jagged boulders. I could tell I wasn't having much to do with this run; I felt the craft's movement coming from the stem and Amanda's powerful strokes. But my feeling of accomplishment was equal to the thrill of going through Pipeline Rapid on a raft. Since my lessons, I've spent many happy hours in canoes on the James—always with one of my expert friends in the stern.

It was on such an outing—we'd paddled upstream to a little sandy beach to picnic and swim—that I saw my first great blue heron. More than three feet tall, it was perched on a rock near our beach. Silently we watched the heron uncurl its long neck and become motionless on its stick legs. Then sighting something we could not see, it folded in its neck and flew swiftly upriver, the long legs trailing behind. The image of that day stayed with me and eventually became the last verse of one of my poems, "At Home Here"—

The rocky James River is out that window, warm
in July it lets me float in my skin among herons.
Or remember a heron, remember its still decision,
and then the act of take-off, of river skim.

One summer day Temple Martin took me downtown—to swim.
We took the downtown expressway to Ninth Street, drove past the
towering Federal Reserve Building and the heart of Richmond's business district to the Reynolds Aluminum parking lot, which is next to
the river. We were going to swim at the end of the Pipeline Rapid.
Temple assures me now that the river had to have been low, three to
four feet that day, and the rapid's series of seven closely spaced drops
nowhere near its possible Class IV rating—or she would never have
suggested the outing.

From the parking lot, we walked though a broken section of
chainlink fence. We climbed onto the pipeline which, for the sake
of workmen—not the fishermen who come to scoop up shad in
nets—has a walkway with railings. Down below we saw a kayaker.
Temple told me that this was the usual takeout for boaters: you
pulled your boat under the pipeline, crossed a shallow canal and
dragged it uphill on a steep concrete walkway into the Reynolds
parking lot. This was the route she had taken after her triumphant
solo canoe run through Hollywood and Pipeline Rapids. (Now the
takeout at the end of the rapids is located on the south side of the
river.) We walked up the river on the pipe until it became just about
the same level as the riverbank, jumped down onto the sand, and
stepped into the water.

That was a day on the James I will never forget. It was a very hot
day, the kind of July heat and humidity that the Tidewater of Virginia
is famous for, that in fact Washington, D.C., residents know too well—
the heavy heat of the south, the humidity of all the waters of swamp
and wetland, the tributaries and streams and rivers headed for the
Chesapeake Bay. The very spot that we waded into is the end of the

James River's cool run of 225 miles from the confluence of the Jackson and Cowpasture Rivers in the mountains of Highland County. Below the fall line, the warm, ever-widening water continues on for 110 miles to the Chesapeake Bay and the ocean.

The water at the base of the rapid was not high but deep enough to immerse ourselves, to float and feel its coolness. We were close enough to the end of Pipeline Rapid to enjoy the show in front of us: a kayak paddler "playing" at the last drop before taking out. Temple explained that, among other games, he was "surfing"—a paddler turns his boat upstream and paddles up to the wave at the end of the rapid; at just the right spot he can remain stationary on top of the wave. To me, he looked suspended by the rushing current, a shad leaping upstream, caught in a photograph.

As we watched the boaters, the birds, hot sunlight on cool water breaking over the last of the prehistoric rocks (the tops of old mountains geologists tell us), Temple reminded me of the phrase, "stone's refusal of the river." It is from a poem by Archibald MacLeish, "What Any Lover Learns":

> Water is heavy silver over stone.
> Water is heavy silver over stone's
> Refusal. It does not fall. It fills. It flows
> Every crevice, every fault of the stone,
> Every hollow. River does not run.
> River presses its heavy silver self
> Down into stone and stone refuses.
> What runs,
> Swirling and leaping into sun, is stone's
> Refusal of the river, not the river.

There we stood in the river, cooled by its last rapids, talking about poetry, watching kayakers—all with the city's skyline immediately behind us.

Though I've never been in a kayak facing upstream, I have learned how to "play" in the water that runs through a city. And as the James River Park System has created more paths, I've found places where you can walk and never suspect you were near a city. I've seen where bald eagles nest—at last returned to our area since fishways have been opened in the dams—and woods dotted with wildflowers and rock walls where beginning climbers learn the skill. I've walked alone or scouted views with an art teacher or talked about imagery with a poetry class. And not long ago, I became a kind of guide to the river myself, as my friends have been for me.

It happened that my friend from Texas, Linda Duncan, came to visit during a winter flood. It wasn't predicted to be a major flood, but the James was roaring and rising. In the late afternoon we set out in my car to go look at the sights where the falls begin. We drove as far as we could along Riverside Drive, then we walked toward the banks and boulders near the Pony Pasture. A dark blue dusk was coming down early and quickly, but we could see, through silhouettes of trees, the coursing, white-capped river. The overflow, its surface shiny in the half-light, had already covered the banks and was lapping across a dip in the road close to where we stood. Wordlessly, taking in this primordial scene, we listened to the pounding current. Suddenly we saw, scurrying across the road, a creature that we have never been able to identify. It seemed to be running but had no legs. It seemed to be a fish, but its skin looked furry. It appeared to be headless, but it was certainly alive. Three years later we confirm these facts to each other, still in wonder, as if we'd witnessed the first air-breathing creature born from water.

And so after three decades of finally getting acquainted with my city's river, it is still a mystery to me. Not a mystery of inaccessibility or of pollutants or of danger, but the mystery of a wild place. What secrets is it hiding? Where did it come from? How will it change? What next? I wonder.

Elizabeth Seydel Morgan is the author of three books of poetry from Louisiana State University Press: *Parties, The Governor of Desire,* and *On Long Mountain.* She has also won prizes for her fiction and a screenplay. She is a graduate of Hollins University and the M.F.A. program at Virginia Commonwealth University. She lives in Richmond and in the Blue Ridge Mountains in Amherst County.

The Nature Conservancy has helped to protect two important natural areas on the James River below Richmond. The Conservancy acquired 3,538 acres and trans-ferred the land to the U.S. Fish and Wildlife Service in 1991 to establish the James River National Wildlife Refuge. The Conservancy also holds a conservation ease-ment donated by the James River Corporation on the 1,756-acre Upper Brandon Plantation.

WHERE RARE PLANTS DWELL
North Landing River

Mary Reid Barrow

Along a ridge of land in the northwestern part of Virginia Beach, a small rivulet changes its flow pattern. Instead of heading toward the Eastern Branch of the Elizabeth River, the little stream begins to make its way south.

As it turns, the North Landing River is born.

From an inauspicious beginning in the heart of Kempsville where it has been made to conform to the backyards, roads and culverts of the most populated area of Virginia Beach, the largest city in the state, the North Landing makes its way toward the city's rural southern half. As it widens and deepens on its course, the little river begins to shine, a star in Virginia's ecological firmament.

Although never much of a river as mighty rivers go, the North Landing more than holds its own on its short run to North Carolina's Currituck Sound. Edged with pristine freshwater wetlands, treed swampland and forested uplands and forbidding to the humans it left behind, the North Landing embraces rare plants, animals and ecological communities found nowhere else in the state.

A vital link in the Intracoastal Waterway, the river is plied by boats going north and south, particularly in spring and fall, yet its marshes still create a home for more rare species in Virginia than any other area east of the Blue Ridge Mountains. This river that snakes down the border between Chesapeake and Virginia Beach continues to astound biologists with its species diversity.

The Nature Conservancy and Virginia's Department of Conservation and Recreation jointly own and manage more than ten thousand acres of rich, swampy habitat that buffers about nine miles of the river's shoreline, thanks to land donations to and purchases by the Conservancy. With almost every exploration of this botanical heaven on earth, biologists discover something rare and wonderful. One day, a discovery could be as large as a virgin forest; another day, something as small as the rare spreading pogonia, a delicate pink orchid. Thus far, more than forty-five unusual or endangered species have been found and scientists are still counting.

The North Landing is designated as one of Virginia's Scenic Rivers, but if you were a passenger cruising the Intracoastal Waterway, you may never come close to understanding this bright star that is carrying you on your journey. Oh, you could get a sense of the peacefulness of the river, disrupted only by sailors and their ilk.

You would see single, stark cypress trees standing like lone waders at the river's edge. You would see osprey in spring and summer, soaring and shrieking on high, and nesting on channel markers and at the very top of waterside tree snags. You may see great blue herons, most probably one of those that nests among hundreds in the largest great blue heron rookery in the state here on the North Landing. You may even see the bald eagle pair that has returned to nest along the river after decades of absence.

Still boaters don't really get to know the North Landing River. To shake hands with the river, you have to meet its wetlands.

Then, you may see colorful freshwater marshes in full bloom in the heat of summer. Giant, showy white rose mallows with their red centers, bright orange flowers of lance-leaved milkweed, and carpets of blue pickerelweed, to mention a few, will knock your socks off.

Then, you can look closely at the waving green grasses that are the canvas upon which the flowers are painted. Among them is sawgrass, a beautiful grass with serrated armor. Indigenous to the Florida Everglades, sawgrass is at its northernmost limit on the North Landing. This tall, coarse reed with its spreading seed heads and golden fall color has made its way up the inland waterway—a protected corridor for plants as for sailboats. Sawgrass is not even found in the nearby freshwater Back Bay, which empties into Currituck Sound cheek by jowl with the river. Touch it gingerly or it will quickly reveal how its serrated edges gave it its name!

great blue heron

If you had slogged into the swamp itself with Conservancy and state scientists one rare June day in 1996, you would have found yourself walking in a virgin forest, never before recorded in botanical annals. Some of the majestic cypress and black gum trees may be as old as eight hundred years. One measured six and a half feet in diameter. These ancient towers of strength comprise possibly the only virgin forest left in Virginia Beach and Chesapeake, but they were a modern-day surprise.

You also may have stumbled upon some of the last stands of Atlantic white cedar in the region. Prized for ships' masts because they grow so tall and straight, the cedars were heavily logged across the southeast many years ago. The North Landing trees were saved from logging by their inaccessible swampy habitat. From on high, the dark green cedars can be seen dominating the tree canopy in some areas.

On that foray, you also may have been intimidated by briar- and bramble-covered pocosins. Pocosins are peat bogs where unusual plants grow, including the pink spreading pogonia. They are among Virginia's most endangered plant communities.

While The Nature Conservancy and the Department of Conservation and Recreation are among the latest to explore this special river, Colonel William Byrd II, an eighteenth-century Virginian, was one of the earliest to be daunted by its dense thickets and enthralled by its beauty. Byrd led a group of commissioners to survey the dividing line between Virginia and North Carolina in the early 1700s. In his diary, Byrd damned the "miry pocosins" that he had to cross. But he also characterized the beautiful grasses growing in the river's vast wetlands as "the Green Sea," an eloquent phrase still used to describe the area today.

One hundred years after Byrd's time, a steam dredge was among the first to tackle the river's marshes again. It fought those very pocosins to dredge a connection from the Elizabeth River to the North Landing as part of the Intracoastal Waterway.

The dredge also dug a channel down the North Landing to Currituck Sound in North Carolina. In the process it made a straight path of the river, dredging through sections of marsh to bypass its natural curves. From on high, one can see the straightened river with its bends off to the side. These castoff river curves are called "oxbows" because they resemble the yoke that goes around an ox's neck.

In those days a writer and illustrator for *Harper's New Monthly Magazine* came down to report on the building of the waterway. He responded in some respects as Byrd had. On the one hand, he raved over the woods of cypress and pine towering over blue flag, coral honeysuckle and sweet-smelling laurel. On the other hand, the writer reported that muskrats "were decidedly in the majority."

The muskrats gained competition as the inland waterway became the route of choice for barges and steamships carrying cotton, fish, wheat, potatoes and lumber from North Carolina to the port at Norfolk, Virginia. In what was Princess Anne County, farmers used tributaries such as Mill Dam and West Neck Creeks and the Pocaty River to reach the North Landing.

Early in the century, a train called the Sportsman's Special brought hunters to the area. The story goes that ducks and geese were so thick on the river and on nearby Back Bay that they could be shot with a cannon. Today, the waterfowl are far less in numbers, but the North Landing still provides a safe resting or wintering spot for birds on the Atlantic Flyway.

Two hundred years after Byrd's time, the "miry pocosins" were still giving visitors fits. Noted botanist Merritt Lyndon Fernald studied the plants along the river in the 1930s and 1940s and complained of the rough going in the tangles and briars of the swamp. But he recognized the diversity of species in the area and concentrated his work there for almost a decade.

Fernald came upon Elliott's aster in the North Landing marshes in the 1930s. It was the first time the tall plant with its pinkish-white flower had ever been recorded in the state. Fernald also came across cranberries growing in the boggy river land. They formed a "carpet," he said, under a stand of sawgrass.

Since Byrd's observations and despite man's altering its course, time has in some ways stood still along this river. The thickets are no less impenetrable and the pocosins, no less miry. Yet modern-day biologists are devoted, as Fernald was, to learning more about this tiny river with a giant presence. They are still looking for cranberries, but they have discovered or rediscovered more than enough species, including the aster, to put it at the top of the list of Virginia's special places.

The river's wetlands shelter not only rare and beautiful plants but unusual animal species as well. The least bittern, a marsh bird that is declining not only in Virginia but across the United States, is one that finds the river's protected habitat to its liking, nesting there in summer.

You may never, ever see the least bittern because it is so good at camouflaging itself. The blackish-buff wading bird can hold its skinny neck and head straight up in the air and become one with the marsh grasses.

You probably will never see the canebrake rattlesnake either, nor may you want to. This poisonous snake is so endangered in Virginia that the North Landing River and Dismal Swamp habitats as well as adjacent areas of Virginia Beach and Chesapeake are the only places it is ever found. This subspecies of its mountain brother, the timber rattler, is fading from the landscape because its habitat has become so overrun by development.

The North Landing is also home to one of the state's largest populations of wood ducks. These beautiful birds nest in tree cavities along lakes, streams and rivers. Their population is declining in areas where old trees have been cut, but along the river, old trees with cavities are a natural part of the landscape.

That goes for the blue heron rookery too. The largest rookery in the state, it provides a nesting area for more than three hundred of the handsome gray-blue herons. They roost in the mature tall trees along the river's forested uplands, welcoming one hundred or so stately great egrets into their safe haven.

A forest near a river provides an ideal habitat for herons because they dine on small fish and crustaceans that live in the shallow marsh waters. More often than not, however, trees near a river's edge are cut to make way for waterfront homes. Not so along the North Landing.

Very few people live along this river. Its swamps and marshes provide little habitat for human housing. The insignificant amount of uplands that actually borders the river's edge floods easily because the river is governed by wind tides. Wind tides occur when southerly winds blow water from Currituck Sound up into the river system. How high the water gets depends on how long the winds blow and how much rain there is. That's one of the reasons that the North Landing has remained a special place for special plants and animals.

The protection provided by the North Landing's swamps and wetlands doesn't make it easy for you to get to know the river on an intimate basis. And The Nature Conservancy and the Department of Conservation and Recreation like it that way to a degree. Threats to water quality along a river in the largest city in the state are very real despite the vast wetlands. So public access is limited. Still there are opportunities to become acquainted by trail, boardwalk and canoe.

On foot, you can come face to face with the wetlands on a Conservancy boardwalk over the marsh. There in summer, brilliant green marsh grasses and swamp plants form a backdrop for equally brilliant wildflowers. Butterflies flit from flower to flower and dragonflies in blues, greens and oranges dart back and forth, popping off the decking or landing and delicately balancing on the very tips of the grasses. Katydids and frogs provide constant background music.

The boardwalk, two-tenths of a mile long, is in bright sun for most of the walk and nature is abuzz in all directions, but a quiet world awaits you at Alton's Creek, another branch of the North Landing, where the state has built a trail and boardwalk. About one-half-mile long, it winds through shadowy swampland and hardwood forest.

There in summer, mossy hummocks loom up out of the swamp and shiny flat green leaves of pennywort dot the seemingly thick, murky water. Brilliant red cardinal flowers along with dappled sunlight are like pathway lights.

Switch cane grows in areas where sunlight penetrates. The grass with bamboo-like leaves gave its name to the canebrake rattlesnake. Like the canebrake, switch cane is another species that has slipped away from most of the state but thrives on the North Landing River.

The rare silky camellia, with its showy dogwood-like blooms that appear in late spring, also grows in this area. Not many places left on earth afford the average person the opportunity to see this beautiful little tree.

Then the boardwalk leads to a trail through a hardwood forest where the canopy of giant old trees prevents any sun from reaching the ground and little if anything lives underneath. The trail ends at a launch, but you have to portage your canoe the whole way. At the end of the trail is a small dock too, just made for contemplating a singular place.

The Nature Conservancy also has built an overlook, reachable only by boat, where Pocaty River and the North Landing meet. There you can get a low-flying bird's-eye view of the marsh and its flowers and critters, another peaceful spot for observing one of Virginia's rare places.

You also can get a bird's-eye view of the river from the high-tech, high-rise Pungo Ferry Bridge, rising sixty-five feet in the air. From on high you will have a view of the North Landing unlike any from down below. You can see how the waterway snaked its way through the marsh before the oxbows were built and, to the north, you can even see one of the oxbows. You look down on the grasses, vibrant green in spring and golden brown in fall and winter. In that one fleeting glance from above, you may get a sense of the past and present of this small river that, despite man's manipulations, has managed to protect so many special species in its watery mantle.

Mary Reid Barrow, a reporter and columnist for the *Virginian-Pilot*, writes mostly about nature and the southern half of Virginia Beach, where the North Landing River is located. In 1997, the Back Bay Restoration Foundation, which works to protect Virginia Beach's southern watershed, gave her its first conservation award.

The Nature Conservancy owns more than seventy-five hundred acres at North Landing River Preserve and, in partnership with the Virginia Deptartment of Conservation and Recreation, has protected a total of more than ten thousand acres on the river since 1990.

In the Blood
Rappahannock River

Walter Nicklin

Watching my two-year-old son's interplay with the world he's found himself in, I get an inkling of insight into first causes. He's fascinated by water. A favorite activity is wading into the shallows of the upper Rappahannock near our home, squatting down to reach the small polished rocks on the river bottom, picking them up, and then dropping them back into the rippling water; each splash brings always a smile, often a giggle. One of his first and most frequent words, however, is neither "river" nor "water"—but "boat."

Which came first? The river or the boat? The Rappahannock, obviously. But in my own consciousness, the two—the river and the means to move with it—are endlessly intertwined.

So, as if building my own vocabulary, I'll start with the boat. More specifically, not just any old boat but one particular old boat, whose age and scarred-with-time body reflect my own. I'll never forget that Christmas morning, now forty some years ago, when my parents, witnessing my politely disguised but still obvious disappointment at the unusually slim pickings under the lighted and decorated cedar, told me to look out the window: there was something Santa had not been able to get down the chimney and so had left outside. What I then beheld—that Christmas of my twelfth year or so—had been the very one thing I'd expressly wished for; and now here it was, on the lawn under a barren oak, with a bright red bow tied on the canoe's middle thwart. Oh, yes, and there were two wooden paddles, also complete with bows, to complete the picture, so perfect I hadn't dared even to imagine the night before. Any doubts about the existence of some kind of Santa Claus were dispelled when I ran out the door into the bitter cold, grabbed a paddle, climbed into the stern seat, and found a comfortable place in a belief, even larger than Santa, that indeed everything could be right with the world.

All that was needed was water. To me, that meant the river. The river with the magical name. The Rappahannock.

In these parts, in those days, canoeing the waters that comprise the upper Rappahannock watershed—the Rapidan, Thornton, Conway, Hughes, Hazel, as well as the main fork of the Rappahannock itself—was considered somewhat radical behavior. Or foolishness, at the very least. On the other hand, lazily fishing from the banks as a form of goal-oriented play was easily understood, even lauded; everybody did it. So, too, at a time when backyard pools weren't so ubiquitous, was swimming—or, more accurately, wading and ducking as a practical way to cool off, since the summertime river was usually too low for any serious swimming holes. But as for canoeing, I remember more than one onlooking farmer chuckling as I dragged the heavy hull across the rocks that blocked my downstream path: "It looks like a lot of unnecessary work if you ask me. You can get wherever it is you want to go a lot faster by walking."

Where did I want to go? On any given day, it might have been Waterloo Landing, Tapp's Ford, Slate Mill, or . . . wherever, it really didn't matter. The point, if there was one, was simply to be on the river, to follow its flow. Wherever it would take me, there was always something to discover around the next bend. To be a woodlands-savvy Indian, exploring frontiersman, or Civil War spy, it was easy to make-believe.

The reality of the Rappahannock itself was what made such fantasy easy. Even the shortest canoe trip was to travel deep into time. Unpolluted (except for agricultural runoff), still free-flowing (except for one dam above Fredericksburg), and its banks undeveloped, the river remained pretty much as it always must have been. That it would ever change was unthinkable. Although I knew there existed villains in the world—like the Army Corps of Engineers, then contemplating another dam at Fredericksburg—I also knew that such evil enemies of Truth and Beauty would surely be vanquished, just as in all the virtuous books I'd read.

kingfisher

And just as I now had to overcome obstacles on my trips down the river: not raging rapids (my parents would have never let me go), but logjams, sandbars, and, most perilous of all, manmade impediments like barbed wire. For the farmers whose land the river ran through, the Rappahannock was not so much a place to play as something to be worked and used, primarily something for livestock to drink from. And to keep cattle from wandering, barbed-wire fences had been strung across the river where it was the shallowest—which usually meant precisely where the rapids were, adding a measure of exhilarating danger to even the mildest of Class I riffles.

If mine was a happy boyhood, the Rappahannock and my canoe—plus the pals who fought with me about who got to sit in the stern—made it so.

* * *

Every child needs some body of water to call his own, though fluid, forever fixed in memory, its currents or tides in the blood. The Rappahannock has helped carry me, I know, during my own figurative journey to the sea. Whenever the world is too much with me, there is nothing a weekend on the river won't put into perspective. There, the waters, even when at flood, are never troubled. Or, when away, just about any waters—no matter where, always somehow, mysteriously reminiscent of the Rappahannock—will do for a cure.

As I write this, for example, I'm sitting on a ramshackle cottage porch in Maine overlooking the rocky shoreline of Casco Bay. To appreciate and contemplate the Rappahannock, it's not necessary to be in a cabin perched on the eastern slope of the Blue Ridge looking down upon the land drained by the river, or a brick Federal townhouse in that old fall-line center of commerce called Fredericksburg, or a plantation terrace downstream toward the Chesapeake near the river's tidal wetlands, some sizable acres of which have been preserved by The Nature Conservancy. I don't feel like a guilty expatriate; any well-watered place evokes the river where I grew up.

It is high tide in Casco Bay, and my son is taking his afternoon nap. By the time he awakes, the tide will be receding, and he will toddle to water's edge—or he'll cry insistently if I won't let him! Like the Rappahannock itself, he is drawn, by some force as strong as gravity, to the Atlantic. There, he will smile as he picks up the still-damp pebbles and tosses them into the gentle waves. He seems to never tire of this lesson in cause and splash that he first learned on the Rappahannock. Occasionally, he looks up for a glimpse of a lobster boat, sailing yacht, or sea kayak, points, and says, "Boat!"

A boat is a boat. The world is one, connected by water. He is not yet able to, or probably even interested in, making adult distinctions. Not old enough to be embarrassed by the aluminum canoe at home, that clunky relic from his father's own youth. He doesn't care that it clangs, that it's not comfortable. Or that, like its kindred cans (of beer and soft drink) in aluminum resting on the river's bottom, it's not environmentally friendly. And that, unlike the sleek lines and molded grace of the fiberglass and polyethylene kayaks and canoes seen everywhere nowadays, it's downright ugly.

So, too, is the Rappahannock, some might say, particularly when contrasted with the picture-perfect beauty of a place like Casco Bay. Certainly, if popularity as a tourist destination is any measure, then the Maine coast in summertime beats the Rappahannock any season of the year. But the natural world is not a beauty contest; besides, love at first sight, as when the Maine fog lifts, is surely not as deeply layered as the affections imprinted from an early age, as I learned to love the Rappahannock.

In the river's very upper reaches, the entangled foliage is so close, it's sometimes as if you can hardly breathe; there is no view—you are in and of the river. Downstream, as the river flattens and broadens before the fall line, the banks change from rocky outcroppings to red clay mud—an eroded eyesore to some, but for a child they make the slickest, grandest waterslides. And what could be more plain and topographically uninteresting than the river's tidal flats—until you look closely, quietly, and long—waiting to watch the insects and the fish and the birds on up the food chain in each patch of marsh grass.

But what of the river's mosquitoes and other biting bugs? Can they ever be loved? It is hard, probably impossible; but they are very good at imparting invaluable lessons, those that can only be learned the hard way.

* * *

I wasn't thinking about mosquitoes when—right around my thirty-third birthday—I set out to travel the Rappahannock from its headwaters atop the Blue Ridge at Chester's Gap to its mouth on the Chesapeake Bay at White Stone. That the trip remains uncompleted, now twenty years later, is certainly nothing to brag about. Still, there's a story here.

It was something I had always wanted to do. That's as good an answer to the "why" of my attempt as the mountainb climber's "because it's there." Although over the years I had "done" every canoeable stretch of the freshwater Rappahannock and its tributaries, as well as sailed and skiffed the tidal river, my intimacy felt like a casual affair, a mere dalliance; my knowledge, fragmentary; there was no unified theory, no integrated personality to what I'd done. Broken into countless different trips at different times, the river was not whole, not one. But, instead, its waters seemed to embody many different rivers, so disparate that their common name "Rappahannock" was the only linkage: little more than a stream in its rocky upper reaches, lined with cliffs and cool-dependent hemlocks; meandering and muddy (with high water) or crystal-clear (with low), as it broadens with the flow of tributaries through manicured farmlands. I had put in and taken out where I wanted, paddled or drifted depending on my mood, jumped in when I got hot. Even the overnight camping trips were short and sweet; even making the necessary hard paddling in the monotonous flat stretches seem, in restful retrospect, like moments of bliss. And on the shuttle back home, to stop at the nearest country store for an ice-cold cola and a chocolate-encrusted Moon Pie brought a pleasure so pure and simple it felt sublime.

But never had I made a long-term commitment to the river I professed to love. To see the course, all 185 miles from the river's source to its mouth, first of all required time, something a working adult has precious little of. At least a week, I reckoned. As it happened, the regional magazine that I had recently launched—whose editorial mission was in part to celebrate the history and nature reflected in special places like the Rappahannock—had run out of money. I had time on my hands, time best used to reflect on what went wrong and what to do next. What better way to do that than tranquilly alone on the Rappahannock?

Not alone, actually. My dog, named Mitty, was perched on the canoe's bow seat. A wiry mongrel that would have looked right at home rummaging for garbage in a city slum, she fancied herself a Chesapeake retriever—tirelessly fetching sticks or balls tossed into the river until the thrower would himself become exhausted. And thus her name, after that greatest of fantasizers immortalized in the story "The Secret Life of Walter Mitty." That my first name was "Walter," too, made the dog and me a fitting pair. With tail wagging in trusting anticipation of the fun times her master had in store for her, she jumped into the canoe with me that June day in 1978 at Crest Hill, as near the river's source as was navigable. Little did she know what in fact awaited us downstream. Certainly, her master, who would betray her trust, had no idea.

That first night we camped, according to my reading of the faded and crumpled topo map that I had brought along from my youth, on a large sandbar just upstream from the old railway town called Remington. Of course, the sandbar itself wasn't shown on the map; nor did it much exist by the time I was awakened the next morning to the sensation of dampness and Mitty's incessant licks on my face. The sandbar had been swallowed by the river in the night. My sleeping bag was soaked, and the canoe was about to float away. There must have been some heavy thunderstorms upstream, and the Rappahannock had lived up to its Indian name, meaning "rapidly rising and falling waters."

The high water meant an easy ride that day, as the current carried the canoe like fast-moving driftwood. I hardly had to paddle. And with many of the rock ledges now underwater, the Class II-III rapids—at Kelly's Ford, Snake Castle, and the confluence with the Rapidan—were a breeze. Happy with my progress, I leisurely and

deliberately picked a campsite for the night: in the woods on a high
bank a few miles above Fredericksburg, although almost within ear-
shot of the I-95 corridor, it was no doubt little changed from when
Yankee pickets might well have used the exact same spot to keep watch
on their Rebel counterparts on the opposite bank. It was easy to
imagine ghosts, oozing from the heavy foliage. Though surely good
ghosts, these Civil War soldiers, Mitty barked and growled all night.
What other unknown creatures lurked outside the lighted perimeter
of our campfire? Virginia versions of the mountain men from James
Dickey's recently published *Deliverance*? My mind played; I got no
sleep—and so began the next day exhausted before I even lifted the
paddle.

We took in water over the gunwales and almost capsized on the
river's very last rapids, which I had canoed countless times before
without mishap, under the Route 1 bridge at the fall line in
Fredericksburg. An omen, perhaps? But we kept going, onto a stretch
of the river I did not know, unexplored, as if I were a frontiersman in
reverse, going backwards in time, discovering what lay around the
next bend downstream instead of up.

And there were bends: on a map, the river here looks like a never-
ending series of hairpins. What with the wind and the incoming tide,
it would probably have been quicker and less strenuous to portage.
That thought first occurred when I was still able to laugh at myself;
later in the day, no doubt in some state of exhaustion-induced de-
lirium, I began to consider it a serious option. Meanwhile, Mitty was
no help at all; whenever she saw any kind of waterfowl (and there
were many), she tried to leap out of the canoe in pursuit. Also dead
weight was the spinnaker rig I'd brought; the winds, too variable, the
river, neither wide nor straight enough. All I could do was paddle.
And paddle. At best I was making about one mile per hour, I figured.
And it was thirty miles to the next bridge, at Port Royal. And after
Port Royal, at least another sixty miles to White Stone. But such
thoughts about the future that lay before me would lead only to the

depths of despair; instead, I had to numb the brain by taking one ever increasingly painful paddle stroke at a time, then another, and another. . . .

And then, as this longest day finally ended—it was in fact right around solstice—the darkness that descended was not the soft light of dusk but heavy black clouds of bugs. The endless night of the hungry mosquitoes had begun. Neither campfire smoke, sprayed repellents, nor netting did any good. Even the poor dog whined, as her soulful eyes said, "How could you?" to the master who had betrayed her. Maybe the river, where a small breeze blew, would offer some relief, I prayed—and packed up all the gear into the canoe and shoved off into the night. And so I paddled all the moonlit night.

By late the next afternoon, when the bridge at Port Royal finally came into view, I had decided to call it quits. And by now the river had straightened, its bends more gradual; so close yet so far was the bridge; I paddled and paddled, as fast as my aching arms would let me; this last mile or so had to be the longest.

* * *

If I have to be beaten at anything, it's best done by a loved and appreciated adversary. Humbled, I can say now that I'm happy the Rappahannock beat me. A mere man, I probably didn't want to triumph over nature. Much better to turn my thwarted energies against my fellow man, in the guise of venture capitalists and reluctant recalcitrant advertisers. So it was that my defeat at the hands of the river inspired me to not give up on my magazine, whose initial failure had given me the time and the excuse to try to tackle the river's length—and for whose subsequent successful twenty-year run I therefore have to thank the gods of the Rappahannock.

So, yes, I still canoe whenever I get a chance; and, of course, I still love the Rappahannock; but when it comes to its mosquitoes, however, "respect" is probably the better word. And one of these days, before I die, maybe I'll complete my unfinished journey. I'll take my son if he wants to go, but our dog Quark, who bears a striking resemblance to Mitty, won't be given a choice. This time I'll be tempted to cheat a bit and use unnatural means of propulsion by bringing along a small outboard motor to bracket on the canoe.

There is one way, I know for sure, that at least some small part of me will finish the trip I never completed—and finally make it to the sea. In my last will and testament, I've asked that my ashes be thrown into the upper Rappahannock. Like the splash of a pebble that makes a child smile.

Walter Nicklin grew up along the banks of the upper Rappahannock, and, though he moved away as a young adult, has since returned to float the river whenever he can. A graduate of Washington and Lee University and the University of Virginia, he has spent most of his professional life in journalism—as a reporter, editor, and contributor for publications like the *Economist,* the *Washington Post,* and the *New York Times*—and in publishing—as an entrepreneur in newspapers, magazines, guidebooks, and catalogs. He is married and has three children.

The Nature Conservancy owns two preserves on the lower Rappahannock River: the 865-acre Alexander Berger Memorial Sanctuary, and the 729-acre Voorhees Nature Preserve, a donation from the Voorhees family in 1994. The Conservancy later acquired 364 more acres just upstream from the Voorhees Nature Preserve and transferred the land to the U.S. Fish and Wildlife Service in 1999 as an addition to the Rappahannock River Valley National Wildlife Refuge.

And This Way the Water
Comes Down at the Gorge
Bullpasture River

Janet Lembke

We gave Charlie to the Bullpasture, his chosen river, on a bright blue, ten-degree day three weeks before Christmas.

No clouds floated on the sky; the distant sun lent a shine without warmth to wet stones and the rushing, braided flow. As always the waters leaped loud and vigorous down their mountain-guarded channel. And on the surface of that fluent noise, smaller sounds bobbed like dry leaves—the scolding of chickadees, the high thin whistles of kinglets. It seemed that the hemlocks and Virginia pines on the riverbank had been decked with living ornaments. Feathers fluffed out, the little birds hovered and hopped, searching the branches for the seeds and dormant insects they need to keep their bodies hot in such cold weather. A shivering day, but the air was filled with clear, clean light. And the occasion held a sense of fitness that could not have been predicted when we planned the trip from town to the mountains and the rolling river.

We'd come here because my mother stubbed her toe. But that's a story for later on. First, I'd like you to see the Bullpasture and how it comes down at its steep-sided gorge.

* * *

Yiii-yi-yi-yi! Yeee-hah!

Yelling their heads off, young'uns mob the summertime river. Male and female, a horde of two dozen teenagers has disembarked from the old blue-painted school bus that's parked up on County Route 678. Surely they raced down the rough plank road that clings to the side of Jack Mountain, the road I've just descended slowly so as not to jostle aging knees. And surely they cast off their clothing without delay. Now, clad in bathing suits and bursting youth, they clamber over rocks, slide screaming down the three-foot waterfall, splash the length of the swimming hole, and climb out to start all over again. Like whirligig beetles, several girls in inner tubes paddle themselves round and round on the calms of the swimming hole. One boy shoots the algae-slick waterfall standing up, arms out for balance, as if he were surfing. The girls cheer. And the fully clothed man standing on my rock notices me and lifts his eyebrows.

Rock? That's too small a word. This wide ledge of ancient gray dolomite veined with subtle pink juts more than a third of the way across the river. Another ledge, equally large, thrusts toward it from the opposite bank. Between them they channel the river's flow into a narrow opening through which it spills down the low, slippery falls where the young'uns are shrieking and sliding. A limestone boulder big as a shed rests squarely in the middle of the opening, almost dividing the falls in two. A boy has climbed on top of it, king of the castle.

I smile. "What fun!"

The man smiles, too. He tells me that he's carried the youth group from church out here, oh, maybe a dozen years now. "But you know, this is the first time there's ever anybody else come down to the swimming hole whilst we was here. Always pick up our trash, we do."

I've made him uneasy. Turns out he doesn't know who owns the land, the state or someone else, and doesn't know if he and the young'uns have any right to be there. The waters, if not the land, are public, but his confusion is understandable. Virginia's Game and Inland Fisheries Department has nailed plastic signs on tree trunks along the road:

TROUT FISHING WATERS
Special license needed for trout in
addition to regular fishing license

Below this legend, an arrow pointing upstream or down, or in both directions, indicates the waters affected by the double-licensing regulation.

These signs give people odd ideas—that the state owns the entire riverbank or that only licensed fishermen are allowed to use the river and its bank. The mere existence of the signs is read as a warning that the land is posted. Truth is, the state does own considerable acreage along this wild bank of the Bullpasture, much of it bought with money from fishing and hunting license fees and managed now for wildlife and forestry. The federal government owns much of the far bank and Bullpasture Mountain rising above it—a sizable tract that's part of the George Washington National Forest. And anyone who wants to can pretty well go traipsing at will—and respectfully—through national forest or the Commonwealth's Wildlife Management Area. But it's not always possible to tell public from private lands, not unless the property is posted, occupied by someone's cabin, or barred by a padlocked gate.

I explain all this to the young'uns' shepherd and tell him, too, that this particular patch of riverbank, the plank road and the rock, belong to me. He and his flock, I assure him, are welcome here. He summons them with a whistle, and off they go.

But they'll be back in their blue-painted bus. Here, in a stony crevice, in a minuscule pocket of soil, a wild rose has taken root, grown, and unfolded one pink blossom. Here in the gorge, the rocks themselves burst into flower.

It's not just young'uns come splashing though this water. So do fish, notably trout. Though Inland Fisheries stocks the Bullpasture, the river still holds fish that were born to its flow, wild fish.

"Native species, oh yes." It's Nevin Davis talking, retired postmaster of Williamsville, the crossroads community that's located just past the downriver end of the gorge where the Bullpasture joins the

Cowpasture. "Last year, young man name of Stone was down by the junction fishing, and he saw something strange in the water, something large swimming and jumping. So he mentioned it to Bobby Lockridge, who was standing on the bank. Bobby got him a stick, waded right into the river, and started using that stick as a club. What he brought out was a brown trout every bit of thirty inches long."

That story would have tickled Charlie.

American chestnut

Near the end of the gorge spring water runs glistening through watercress and bullrushes down to the river. A wall of river stones was long ago built around the spring to create a pool from which the ice-cold water can easily be dipped. Access to this water probably accounts for the location of Charlie's cabin. It's not an unmerciful chore to tote full buckets a mere hundred feet.

Charlie didn't exactly build the cabin. He christened it, though, and called it Spit 'n' Whittle after two male pastimes of long and honorable

standing. But my mother, his sister, called the cabin The House That
Jack Built, not because it was the trigger for a series of disasters but
because a man named Jack Marshall had sold Charlie the land and
helped him reconstruct an old log cabin first raised in the nineteenth
century. They built a new fireplace and chimney of river stones.
Bullpasture Mountain's oak trees gave them shakes for the roof, and its
chestnuts, the split rails for the fence around the cabin's clearing.

These things occurred when Charlie was in his twenties, before the
chestnuts were wiped out by blight, before World War II swept him up,
a captain in the National Guard, and sent him to Omaha Beach.

But in those years that he was gone for a soldier, years that also put
my father in an Army uniform, cabin, clearing, and cool-welling spring
did not languish but were put into the keeping of women and children. Whenever my mother could save, beg, or borrow enough gas-
rationing coupons for the fifty-mile trip from town to the Bullpasture
gorge, she packed us all up—my two brothers and me, our grandmother and her English springer spaniel—and gave us transport to
The House That Jack Built.

From the instant of arrival till return to town, we played. I didn't
see it then as play—or as a temporary, adult-engineered shrugging
off of war. For me, everything we did was part of daily life. And if we
did things we didn't do in town, like spitting in the yard when we
brushed our teeth, we were simply following the river's dictates. And,
oh, the games the Bullpasture had to offer: wading, turning over rocks
to catch crayfish, pole fishing, climbing atop the limestone boulders,
zipping down the algae-slick waterfall, and loafing through the reaches
of the swimming hole. The place I liked best was a big rock ledge
jutting into the river. Its surface bore lichens of palest peach and gray
and green. Ferns curled upward from its soil-filled crevices, along with
grasses and even some saplings. Ants, beetles, and spiders lived among
them, and swallowtail butterflies flitted overhead. Below the water
line snails crawled in their conical black shells, and minnows darted.
I named the rock Mother Nature.

At that time and in that remote mountain hollow, we might well have been in the nineteenth century. War had largely deprived us of automobiles, and the cabin had never been fitted out with town's amenities—electric lights, water from a tap, an indoor toilet. A one-hole outhouse served us, and the cooking was done on a wood stove. My mother walked to the Williamsville country store for food and used a shoulder yoke to tote buckets of sweet water from the spring. Wearing a sunbonnet, smoking a corncob pipe, my grandmother sat on the front porch and supervised. We kept darkness at bay with candles and flashlights and, on mountain-chilly evenings, a crackling fire on the hearth.

But in 1943, I was sent away to summer camp, and away again in 1944. That was the year of Charlie's return home. In 1945, my father came back from the war and moved his family north, unreachably far from the silent water welling and sparkling in the clear spring, far from the tumultuous water tumbling and rushing down at the Bullpasture's five-mile-long gorge.

* * *

A river of cattle surges down the dirt road. Some are solid red, some red and white, and still others roan. All have large, sharp-pointed horns. The herd's animals, more than a hundred strong, low and bawl and roll their eyes. Onward they plod, and dust rises from their hooves in billowing clouds. Several men on horseback accompany the herd. Riding at the sides or in the rear, they chivvy it onward. But no mounted cowboy sets the herd's pace. That task is performed by a footman, who holds the sturdy lead ropes that are tied to the flaring horns of the two steers right behind him. He walks, they follow. They've crossed through Panther Gap down at Goshen. Another day and the drive from the valley to summer pasture will be over. The return to a lowland farm won't take place till November or December.

That's how it was in the 1850s. The drives from the lowlands over Panther and Buffalo Gaps and up into the lush mountain valleys continued through the first two decades of the twentieth century. One of Charlie's sisters, not my down-to-earth mother, but the other one, the dreamy sister, recalled accompanying their Uncle Willie as he took his cows from the farm down on Middle River for summer grazing up in Highland County near Monterey. That drive occurred in the days of the First World War. And cattle are still being driven from farm to farm in the vicinity of Monterey, though the phenomenon is much reduced in size, with only small herds mooing and shuffling for a few miles along a county road.

Bullpasture, Cowpasture, and, yes, Calfpasture. Each flows through its own valley to make a trio as magically complete as any congeries of three, from the three bears to the Trinity. The springtime cattle drives afford one explanation for the placing of such names on the land. Beginning with calves and ending with bulls, it holds that the three river valleys, with their fine grazing, were named for the order in which the animals tired on the long trek to the highlands.

Charlie once kept a cow. That was in postwar days, after he'd taken a wife and sold his cabin. He named her Twiddles because that was what he did to her udder in order to milk her.

But it likely wasn't cattle that figured in the naming of the three rivers and their valleys.

The Bullpasture wells ice-cold out of ancient rock up there close to the crest of Jack Mountain, which rises near the West Virginia border. Down the mountainside it trickles, slowly at first but with increasing thrust as it gathers in water from tributary springs and brooks. It races and tumbles down to its wide floodplain, and there, with Jack Mountain on the west and Bullpasture Mountain on the east, it begins to dawdle. Now winding this way, now wandering that, it takes its own clear, sweet time to meander the twenty miles down to the gorge. And the valley through which it loafs is a green lake of grass. Sheep drift in woolly clouds across its treeless surface, and cattle graze. This valley, like its two counterparts, is pasture indeed. It has provided pasturage for millennia.

Imagine autumn. Imagine fire. Not only are the mountainsides ablaze with gold and scarlet leaves, but real flames lick at the stiff, frost-killed meadow grasses. Purposely kindled, fanned by a rising wind, the many little fires grow and join forces, burning the valley floor from end to end. In spring new shoots will poke up fresh and green through the blackened earth. And the herds of bison will return to graze and grow fat. It is Indians—Shawnee, Cherokee, Delaware—who put the dry grass to the torch each year as soon as hunting season ends, so that the river valley stays clear of trees and thus continues to invite annual pasturage by these most excellent providers of meat, hides, sinews, and bone, these great shaggy sources of life.

By 1800, the bison were gone from western Virginia. Fifty years before that, white settlers had begun bringing red cattle into the mountain valleys. The English names that were given to the valleys in the 1700s did not speak, however, of domestic livestock but rather of the larger bovine that had grazed immemorially in river-sweetened meadows. Calfpasture, Cowpasture, Bullpasture—the valleys were named first, and their names later slipped onto the rivers. But first the Cowpasture was Clover Creek and the Bullpasture, Newfoundland Creek.

Terror swept down at the gorge the summer I was twenty.

By then, Charlie was an insurance salesman living with wife, Twiddles, and sundry goats on a farm close to town. Though he no longer owned cabin and clearing, spring and Mother Nature rock, they hadn't slipped out of the family. My father had bought the place. College, however, had kept me on the far side of the Mason-Dixon line. But in the freedom of early summer, I brought a friend to stay at Spit 'n' Whittle so that she could see for herself that my talk about the Bullpasture was not hyperbole but rather an inadequate approximation of the cool, wet, ever-rushing truth. In the afternoon of a blue and gold June day, we'd put on bathing suits and sneakers, grab up sturdy sticks, and go for a river walk. But walking was soon traded for soaking up sun. We each chose a river boulder, climbed aboard, and stretched out.

Of the three rivers, all are cradled in mountain valleys, all meander across the wide meadows, but only the Bullpasture thrusts down a gorge as it looks for the sea. Five miles above its junction with the Cowpasture, the mountains on either side of its floodplain slam almost shut. From that point till it reaches its sister river, the Bullpasture is locked by steep, forested cliffs into a tightly constricted channel. Shadows linger here in the morning and return early in the afternoon. Mountain walls permit the full entry of sunlight only at midday. Always that steep-sided canyon prisons the river as it carries its burden. And sometimes there's more water than the space available can handle. When spring rains come pouring down, or brief but torrential summer thundershowers, water may saturate the soil of the Bullpasture's upper valley. The river rises, overflowing its pebbled bed, and the meadows drown beneath a sprawling flood. Obeying gravity's pull, the flood rolls downhill and enters the rockbound narrows of the gorge.

Terror was barely audible at first. It began as a distant rumble superimposed on the river's incessant rush. And the unplaceable sound grew larger, louder, closer.

No time for fear. No time for thought. We first saw the water as it rounded a bend two hundred yards upstream—a wall five feet high, turbid, frothing, all a-roar. It bristled with deadwood. It hurtled at us. Then it crashed over us, careless and swift.

I don't know how we had the wit to grab our sticks, nor how we hung onto them as we were torn loose and tossed downstream. But wedged between stones on the riverbed, the sticks became upright posts to which we clung. We were safe then.

The odd part was that there'd been no indication that terror would sweep down the summer river. The skies had been cloudless; no thunder warned of storms upstream. I conjecture decades later that a farm impoundment or perhaps a beaver dam had been breached. It is fact, however, not conjecture, that my first intimation of mortality came down at the gorge.

Flux is the order of the day, the year, the millennium, and always has been. The iron suspension bridge that linked the Spit 'n' Whittle side of the river with Williamsville on the west bank has been replaced with a concrete model. The village itself has almost disappeared, though Nevin Davis grumbles justifiably that traffic and highway trash have both increased. Weekdays, only the post office, still open for business, holds the village designation in place; on Sundays, the minister and congregation of the old red-brick Presbyterian church tend to that task.

Charlie saw little of the changes. The need to earn a living took him away not just from Twiddles and his farm but from the Shenandoah Valley. His death in the mid-seventies took place east of the mountains on alien soil. It was several years later that he finally came home. His widow gave his neatly packaged ashes to my mother, who stored them in a closet and forgot they were there. Nor did she remember until, at the end of the eighties, she moved from a very large house to more manageable quarters.

Yet some things seem by nature or circumstance resistant to change. One is Spit 'n' Whittle. The rough dirt lane is smoothed, and the woods have been allowed to encroach beyond the now-sagging split-rail fence. Astonishingly, some chestnuts have regenerated enough to bear fruit; the yard is littered in fall with prickly hulls. But as the twentieth century rushes pell-mell toward the twenty-first, the cabin reconstructed by Charlie of nineteenth-century logs stands foursquare and sturdy. It's now the property of the Beaver Falls Hunting Club—refugees from the crowded flatlands near Washington, D.C. In November after stalking deer, they warm themselves at a fire that crackles on the river-stone hearth set in by Charlie. The branch water in their bourbon comes from the spring at which my mother used to fill her yoke-borne pails. The spring still wells up clear and icy-cold; the overflow still trickles to the river; a path still follows the riverbank to the big, lichen-covered rock.

If anything has been granted immunity from change, it's the river. Though the structures built by people rise and fall, and people themselves live, work, and die, the river has endured like an unspoiled gift, a natural truth. There's been a recent threat, however: in the early 1990s, turkey growers made incursions into the Bullpasture's valley. But now, at the turn of the century, Roger Canfield, of the Mountain Soil and Water Conservation District, assures me that restrictions were put in place before massive poultry operations could taint the river with their leachates. The number of turkey farms upstream has been limited to fourteen, each monitored on an individual basis.

The river still runs true. Its water comes down at the gorge with clean white noise as necessary and calming and close to silence as a steady pulse. It is still the same changeable yet changeless water that comforted my youth.

* * *

"When shall we go to the river?" my mother asked not long before Thanksgiving.

"After the holidays," I said, "after life settles down."

"No, now. Ashes in my closet, you see—they're just not convenient." Her tone was peremptory. She pointed to her left foot and told me that her toes were bruised because, when she'd gone that morning to select clothes, her toes had suddenly banged into Charlie. Awaiting who knows what occasion, he'd been stored for a dozen-plus years in one closet or another, from the huge walk-in model in her very large house to the small, unfamiliar bedroom cubicle in the small, manageable dwelling she'd recently leased. Where to put him? We could take Charlie nowhere but to his river in the gorge between Bullpasture and Jack Mountains.

And in frigid, bright December, we went there, my mother, my elder brother, and I. My brother carried Charlie down the logging road. We'd opened the package in the car and left its outermost cardboard carton there. The carton had held a sturdy box of dark-brown plastic that in turn contained a heavy-duty plastic bag closed with a twist tie and filled with light gray, almost silvery powder. Brown box in one hand, my brother used the other to steady our mother, fragile and cautious with the weight of eighty years. With slow ceremony we made our way down and down, the river sounding its processional uproar, the kinglets and chickadees singing a descant.

She stood on the riverbank watching as my brother and I walked out on my rock. There, near the waterfall, we linked arms and gave Charlie to his river. The ashes swirled, spreading out in a milky cloud. Astonished by joy, we gazed at them until they disappeared.

Bullpasture pours down into its sister stream. Cowpasture descends into the James, the James into Chesapeake Bay, and thence to the ever-surging pastures of the sea.

And this way the water comes down at the gorge.

Janet Lembke is a natural historian and the author of five books of natural history: *Dangerous Birds, Shake Them 'Simmons Down, River Time, Looking for Eagles,* and *Skinny Dipping.* A translator of Greek and Latin, she divides her time between her home in Staunton, Virginia, and the banks of North Carolina's lower Neuse River, where she and her husband live happily in his riverside trailer.

ABOUT THE EDITOR

Robert M. Riordan is the director of communications for the Virginia Chapter of The Nature Conservancy. He lives in Charlottesville, Virginia. This is his first book.